DOWNTOWN

MICHAEL MUSTO

VINTAGE BOOKS
A Division of Random House
New York

A VINTAGE ORIGINAL,
FIRST EDITION May 1986

Copyright © 1986 by Michael Musto

All rights reserved under International and Pan-American Copyright Conventions. Published in the United States by Random House, Inc., New York, and simultaneously in Canada by Random House of Canada Limited, Toronto.

Library of Congress Cataloging-in-Publication Data

Musto, Michael, 1955–
  Downtown.

  "A Vintage original"—T.p. verso.
  1. New York (N.Y.)—Social conditions. 2. New York (N.Y.)—Social life and customs. I. Title.
HN80.N5M87 1986   306'.09747'1   85-40667
ISBN 0-394-74285-0

Front cover photographs of woman and car by Nan Goldin; photograph of man by Patrick McMullan. Jewelry courtesy of Einstein's.

Cover design by George Corsillo.

Book design by Cynthia Eyring

Manufactured in the United States of America

To my parents, Ciro and Anna Musto

«Acknowledgments»

William Love, Mary Kaye Schilling, Michael Small, Bobby Breslau and my wonderful editor, Jayne Nomura

Contents »

1 "You're on the Guest List . . ."/1

2 "Let There Be Downtown"/11

3 "East of Eden, North of SoHo"/23

4 "Low Rent, High Society"/35

5 "Living It Up and Never Living It Down"/53

6 "All Dressed Up with Everywhere to Go"/83

7 "Come Up and See My Etchings . . . No Seriously"/101

8 "Curtain Up . . . Where Are the Lights?"/123

9 "The Not So Defiant Ones"/141

10 "And the Beat Goes On"/159

1

«You're on the Guest List...»

At Limelight's "June Bride" event, held in the summer of '84, a swarm of downtown desperados turned up to be part of the wedding party. Few of the "brides" wore white. Even fewer were real women.

When you're alone and life is making you lonely, you can always go downtown . . . if you're on the list. (Preferably the "A" list.)

Oh sure, anyone can hop into a Porsche—or a Sherman tank—and drive through the chicest rubble in town to gape and gawk at New York's young, gifted and broke, but to go beyond touristy and be welcomed into the downtown elite, you have to observe a few thousand rules. First, realize that there *are* no rules; you just look and do as you feel. Second, be incredibly rebellious and angry, but not to the point where it might hurt your career. Walk around with a huge chip on your shoulder, but only if the chip looks fabulous. Feel a constant, driving creativity—rather than throw out a beer can, you should feel the urge to make an earring out of it. Above all, get bored so easily that by the time a trend you started becomes accepted, you should be willing to let someone else cash in on it just so you can move on to the next three trends. Always be a member of the vanguard, even if you have to pay dues to join.

The downtown scene is so transient that just as you discover a club, you find it's been turned into a pizzeria, but that's okay; wait fifteen minutes and it'll be a club again. There's such a need for constant stimulation that hair salons have art on the walls and art galleries can have hair on the walls if they like. Clubs become showrooms, American Legion offices become clubs, and the only thing certain is that nothing is certain. Roller discos suddenly change into gay Arab-biker sushi bars just for the sake of change, and no one questions the transformation as long as free drink tickets are still available. One club, Area, makes its reputation largely on the fact that it changes its theme and decor from top to bottom every five or six weeks, so even though it's always the same old thing, once in a while it becomes a whole new same

- Many are called, but few are chosen. On a good night the crowd outside Area makes *The Day of the Locust* look like a scout camping trip. Push, but not too hard—some of the people you're pushing may be doormen at other clubs.

old thing. Other clubs pride themselves on the fact that they change their decor every single night. It's possible for a club to span the entire history of humankind, from a biblical party on Monday to a 2010 party on Sunday—though you'd better have the appropriate outfit for each time span or you'll become history yourself. And don't forget the outer garment required for Vito Bruno's "outlaw" parties at such unlikely outdoor events as subway station entrances and bridge promenades. These open-air extravaganzas promote both the layered look and the prompt start—everyone shows up on time, knowing full well the event will be busted by midnight—usually giving people a solid ninety minutes of nerve-racking fun.

Downtown parties are exercises in sensory stimulation. A rat put in a hot club instead of a Skinner box would probably go borderline psychotic from all the fabulous stimuli. Club regulars have seen it all, and want more. Just dancing is boring, especially since no one dances anymore, and dancing with video monitors in the background is irritating, especially since a video you don't like could put your dancing feet to sleep. But dancing with video and live bands and fashion shows and art installations might hold some people's attention until the next complimentary cocktail comes along. The clubs, with all these elements thrown together, are a microcosm of the whole outlandish mish-mosh that is downtown, a best-of-the-wildest vaudeville revue that starts at midnight and ends when everyone feels like it.

This mercurial quality has given downtown a fascinating luster as insiders and outsiders alike knock each other down to discover a trend that might still be viable by five-thirty. Downtown has caught the public's imagination so intensely that many people are content just to observe this three-ring circus of bearded fashion victims, fake unicorns with swelled heads grafted on and incredibly acrobatic young creative types from afar—it's less exhausting that way. Mainstream America is fascinated with the idea of a scene in which seemingly everyone is an artist, musician, designer or "beauty engineer" (i.e. a hairdresser) and keeps such unusual office hours—from dusk to dawn. The media has latched onto and glorified the scene's peculiarities, making yesterday's societal outcasts today's luminaries of fashion and fabulousness. This wasn't always the case. Except for an occasional "Real People" segment on someone with pink hair, downtowners had long been left to their own devices in the relative obscurity of the Lower East Side. But as these outcasts became noticed, their image ascended from that of freaks to that of freaks with talent, with mixed results. The Felliniesque cast of characters was finally accepted, but along with that acceptance came crass commercialism in the guise of gentrification. The neighborhood they created in the Lower East Side was invaded by not very creative franchises and money-hungry real estate agents.

That's one of the paradoxes of the

downtown scene—the more recognition it gets, the less of a definable entity it becomes as outside forces pounce on it and put it out of the financial range of the people who prompted the whole scene in the first place. *People* wrote about it in the summer of 1984 and rents went up. *Life* covered it in the summer of 1985 and by then the scene was so ready to be shipped for mass consumption, it's a wonder creativity was still part of the package. But despite their surface anti-authoritarian attitudes, a lot of downtown people would love a crack at fame and a chance to go mainstream, even if it means their environs are losing a little bit of funk appeal. "Gentrification!" many of them scream as they arrange their press clippings into neat little portfolios.

The battle between rebelliousness and career ambitions helps make downtown a hotbed of volatility. The fact that every day there's a whole new legion of artists, musicians and designers—Where do they come from?—keeps everyone on his and her creative toes. If you don't continually push and innovate, you could find yourself a has-been in your early twenties, enjoying a cup of mud ("Clink, clink, darling!") with the local degenerates, which is not as appalling as it may sound. Even the local degenerates have attained a patina of semi-chic—they seem to be destroying themselves in more glamorous ways than before. Fortunately, they're outnumbered by the artists, and the artists are outnumbered by people interested in their art. Curiosity about the scene has reached such a feverish pitch that when Cyndi Lauper—rock's queen of glad rags and crazy colors—revealed to the world that some of her brilliantly hideous ensembles of bargain wear were procured at various downtown thrift shops, people started shopping in this long-ignored area for their own perfect mismatches. When Keith Haring and Jean Michel Basquiat, one-time bad boys of public chalk and spray-can statements, started commanding high five-figure prices for their paintings, the downtown scene went over the top. It wasn't just chic anymore, it was profitable, and that makes it chicer than ever.

In fact, downtown's so chic it's not just downtown anymore. It's a feeling, a style, a sensibility that's invaded popular culture, no matter where it might be located. No longer do downtowners get nosebleeds above 14th Street, now they're pretty safe all the way up to 23rd and maybe even beyond that. Department stores feature downtown-style displays. Large magazines prey off the glamor and vogue of downtown mademoiselles while avant-garde publications skyrocket from Avenue A to Madison Avenue. Formerly subterranean personalities appear in MTV videos and East Village annoyances become international superstars. Suddenly the scene is turned into what cynics might liken to one big Haring canvas of faceless creatures feeding off each other until everyone has hollowed-out middles. But at least the canvas is worth five-figures.

You come to realize just how loose

● Francine Hunter enjoys a rare moment of repose at Jungle Red, her hair salon, where the new-style entrepreneur deals in art, accessories, fashion and, of course, hair styling.

the geographical parameters of the scene are when you learn that one of Lauper's favorite "downtown" vintage clothing shops is Screaming Mimi's, on the Upper West Side. As spiraling rents force a lot of young artists out of the Lower East Side, downtown becomes anywhere they can get a reasonable apartment, even if that includes Hoboken, New Jersey, or Long Island City, Queens—places they would have retched at a few years ago. Downtown is a state of mind so fabulous that, until there's a guest list for public transportation too, all it needs to travel is a token.

According to Francine Hunter, who's owned and run Jungle Red, a highly successful hair salon since 1977, "Downtown is a style that uptown has had to cultivate to keep inside the competition and be au courant. Six years ago I knew there'd be something happening down here—it's more relaxing, individualistic and creative. There's more of an exchange between the clientele and the person dealing the product. That's what people enjoy about buying now. They don't want to be told or sold. They want to feel comfortable and enjoy some personal interaction. There are a lot of independent businesses down here where that kind of interaction can happen.

"The development of SoHo in the seventies led to a merging of music, fashion and fine art. Suddenly, there were many things you could do independent of form. You didn't have to work for a big magazine or Barney's or apprentice for Calvin Klein. In the past seven or eight years, people have taken the risk of being independently supported instead of the classic, 'I have to work for Sassoon to become a hairdresser' routine. From seventy-six to seventy-nine, people came here and cultivated a different approach That's given downtown its character and its edge."

Hunter's certainly cultivated a different approach. A former stripper and go-go dancer, she says she developed a lot of entreprenurial smarts in burlesque. "I learned a lot about business, style and theater in those years. I knew if I opened my own business, it would be just like a whorehouse, only selling something different, and in a more humane and compassionate way." Her skills have paid off; people are so aroused by the hairdressing (not to mention the collection of couture women's wear, Japanese toys, Brazilian festival clothing, accessories and art that also populate her multimedia space), Hunter's built up a clientele that goes beyond just downtown. "The kids that start the trends don't spend the money," she says from experience. So, she's developed a diverse patronage that comes for the esoteric atmosphere and are open-minded enough to want her "colorful, sometimes wild" styles. "But I know people's limits," she adds shrewdly. Like anyone trying to carry on a business, she knows that trends and outrage come and go, but classic things like certain minor sex-related ailments are forever. The best businesses anywhere don't suffocate themselves with exclusivity.

"Everybody wants to make it uptown

● New York's subways are often locations of terror, but when party-thrower extraordinaire Vito Bruno took over the entranceway to one in '85, the only terror was that the fabulous (but illegal) bash would end.

in the real world," says Alan Rish, a party-giver who feels everything is "dead," except his own parties. "It's good to be cute and downtown, but if you don't make it in the real world, you're not as amusing as the years go by.

"A lot of the dress-up-and-party people object to uptown. Many times I won't even invite downtowners to some uptown events because they'd go, 'Ugh, debs!' or 'Socialites!' But the downtown people I respect most like uptown. It's all being fused together anyway. People like Janis Savitt, Marcus Leatherdale and Larissa are uptown, but they're downtown too. Teri Toye may have been downtown, but she's jet-setting all over the world and modeling in big designer shows. Way Bandy has to deal with twenty-thousand-dollar-a-day shootings, but his sensibility is really downtown. What do you call Scavullo, who appreciates both elements?" (Most people call him Mr. Scavullo, but his good friends call him Francesco. And no one calls him late for dinner, whether we're talking up or down.)

The fascination may go both north and south, but the thrill of downtown is still the newest and most exciting of recent New York phenomena. A lot more people want to get in than get out. "Right now the entire world is focused on downtown," says Vito Bruno. "It's a major force. You put those key downtown names on an invitation and everybody wants to come down and check it out."

See it, enjoy it, absorb it—and make sure you're on that "A" list. If not, settle for the "B" list. And if those snobby club doormen tell you you're not on any list, threaten to ruin them with just one phone call. If that fails, scream at the top of your lungs, "Don't you know who I was?" (Modesty works sometimes, only if it's false.) Welcome to downtown.

«Let There Be Downtown»

The Mudd Club was downtown's answer to the glitz and glamor of uptown clubs like Studio 54. There were no glitter balls, smoke machines or free drink tickets, but the unpretentious, out-of-the-way "dump" was strangely chic, attracting types as diverse as lawyer Roy Cohn *(left)* to suburban punks *(right)*— and everything in between. Downtown society may well have begun the first time owner Steve Mass let in a South-of-Houston notable for free.

Like day camps, where kids get to flaunt all their skills from mouth organ to macrame, the clubs are showcases for all of downtown's arts and abilities, from the performances on stage to the music coming from the d.j. booth to the fashion that fills every crevice. In the clubs all the creative fields publicly converge to be noticed and mutually influenced.

Downtown's evolution has been mirrored in the shiny surfaces of every new club; as the scene changes, so does *the seen*—the nightlife—and vice versa. All the rumblings of alternative culture that started on the Lower East Side streets and in little boutiques, galleries and impromptu rehearsal halls joined forces in places like the Mudd Club to make the giant explosion that became downtown.

Some contend that it officially started when Mudd owner Steve Mass ("Dr. Mudd") decided to let certain scenemakers into his club for free. They weren't famous, but Mass acknowledged these upstarts were broke yet important to the club because they were creatively volatile. They were the Debbie Harrys and David Byrneses of the future, presuming they could survive the afterhours lifestyle for more than another week.

Was that the beginning? Actually, it was more the beginning of the legitimization of the scene. By comping the creative types, Mass was giving them celebrity treatment no one had imagined for them except maybe themselves. At Studio 54, Halston and Raquel Welch were big names, but at the Mudd, it was all about Animal X, Colette, Hal Ludacer and other luminaries of the Lower East Side who's who, all of whom were considered strictly "Who cares?" by uptown.

But the downtown scriptures start way beyond that. Anyone who's been around long enough and is willing to admit it points to Micky Ruskin's Max's Kansas City as the early high point of downtown. "A fragile, astonishingly historic coalition of life, beauty, art, comedy, drama, glamor, sex, fame and fun" is how one regular, rock-manager-turned-magazine-editor Danny Fields, put it. "If you dropped your keys in the back room and went to pick them up," says another wag who frequented the place, "you saw half of New York having sex." The other half was busy dropping keys.

Max's was where Andy Warhol superstars mingled with real people who even mingled with some real superstars. People seemed to change genders just in the course of a drink, and some even changed careers in *search* of a drink, while others caroused, danced on tabletops and made public fools of themselves, then waited to become famous for it. The club was a forecast of the scene to come—loose, individualistic and full of people trying to stretch their fifteen minutes of fame into a full half hour. It was such a forecast that a lot of the same people are still on the scene today (and some of them still won't say hello), though they now show up more out of obligation than desire. "That time was magical," says syndicated rock columnist/TV personality Lisa Robinson, waxing nostalgic about the good old seedy days at Max's and another club called the Scene. "Now, places get co-opted too quickly by people who consciously want to be trendy. New York has become *New York Magazine*. I still go out because rock is connected with nightlife and style, but I don't feel like I'm missing something if I don't go out. If you missed a night at Max's, you were *missing* something."

Another Max's regular, Susan Blond (a Warhol favorite who's now his favorite Epic Records VP), says, "Then, the people were really interesting. Now, they try to be interesting. But every generation feels their scene is the best. For me, Max's and Studio 54 were absolutely thrilling. The *New Yorker* first wrote about me as 'Susan Blond, who's famous at Max's,' which was a claim to legitimate fame in itself. I'd walk into the back room—I don't even know what I'd done—and I'd get a standing ovation. That's how I like to be treated." Everyone was a star at Max's; if you were smart enough to be there in the first place, you had to be a somebody.

When Studio 54 opened in April of 1977 on the site of a large, expensively renovated TV studio, the nightlife focus changed from crud to glitz, from attitudinizing and mingling to spinning on the dance floor and knocking people over, from minimal fashion statements to designer chic. Even the drag queens seemed to be getting more extreme as their wigs reached dangerous new heights. This was not a place downtown treasured. It was too hyped and shiny and the disco drone led to one big downtown headache. Besides, the Lower East Side wasn't exactly swept in the door. The disco era was too self-absorbed to consider the next wave.

While the lights whirled, confetti shot out of little cannons and people acted out "Don't Leave Me This Way" in layered chiffon (the guys) and three-piece suits (the girls) as a half-moon with the biggest coke spoon attached descended upon them. Unfortunately, most people were too preoccupied with their own life-sized silverware to catch it. At the same time, oblivious to all this beep-beep-toot-toot, a group from Athens, Georgia, called the B-52's was playing to an audience of about twenty at a small, funky place called 77 White Street. This hole-in-the-wall was nestled in the middle of absolutely nowhere safely below Canal Street and off a deserted, flooded, smelly side street. It was fabulous. Particularly that night, because the B-52's with their glorified white-trash look, replete with polyester bellbottoms and beehive wigs, were bopping to the nervous, hilarious sound that would ultimately make them kitsch and famous. And it continued to be fabulous after that because by the time Steve Mass had named the place the Mudd Club, it had become the Studio 54 of the alternative crowd. The kind of crowd that would feel more at home socializing in a pud-

● Even outside Max's Kansas City, the party was exhibitionistic and intense. The club was a forecast of downtown to come—but few people that night were thinking of the future.

dle of indefinable fluid than slaving in a pool of indistinguishable secretaries in an office.

Just like at Studio 54 and practically every other club in town, it was in the bathroom where the most intense sex, drugs and rock and roll took place at the Mudd. But there was something else besides all that. A wild cacophony of artists, designers and musicians were there every single night. Their sensibility was narrow ties and open minds, minimalism and maximum attitude, androgyny, asexuality and ambiguity along with a heavy sense of "We Are the World" that had nothing to do with charity. "Everyone was so cool," recalls designer Dianne Brill, "and everyone went home alone."

Fresh off the punk hype, the media was quick to label the latest movement "new wave," but that nebulous term could just as well have been supplanted by anything from "post punk" to "spunk rock" to "tidal wave" to "wave bye-bye." Whatever you called it, it was one giant step away from punk, which was an expression of righteous indignation about everything, including indignation itself, led by a brigade of leather-clad youths who hadn't felt happy about anything since the doctor slapped their bottoms at birth. They wore that unhappiness on their (dirty) lapels like some kind of reverse status symbol. The new wavers took punk's rebellious anger and made it more aesthetically pleasant. They strived less to nauseate than to arouse with their ragged energy. When Blondie's Debbie Harry went from wearing a blood-stained wedding gown at CBGB's to wearing hot pants and singing the melodic, danceable (if lyrically biting) "Heart of Glass," the group became international new wave darlings. Unlike punks, new wavers were perfectly willing to restructure their neuroses into hit records.

The Mudd brought those neuroses to dizzying multimedia heights. Most of the guys looked like Anthony Perkins and the girls looked like MacKenzie Phillips. Bands like the Lounge Lizards and James White and the Blacks played furious jazz-rock on the main floor,

VIP's looked at (and became) bizarre installations on the second floor, and soon the third floor became the Mudd art gallery, showing the work of future legends such as Kenny Scharf, Jean Michel Basquiat and Fab Five Freddy. They and other artists realized that a show in a club instead of a gallery didn't spell career suicide. In fact, Keith Haring got some of his first notices when he did a show in 1980 at Club 57, a wild and woolly hangout/gallery/performance space at 57 St. Marks Place. It had been the basement of Holy Cross Polish National Church before it became what has been described by writer Steve Hager (*Beat Street* author) as a cross between a thirties Berlin cabaret and a fifties sock hop.

Both the Mudd and Club 57 broke rules, and hearts, especially if you weren't accepted into their airtight social hierarchies. Ruled by their own cliques of legends-in-their-own-minds, they accorded so much importance to social status that an actress/scenemaker named Tina L'Hotsky actually had herself crowned Queen of the Mudd in a very serious coronation ceremony. Later that evening, she went back to her dingy apartment.

"I didn't have time to compete with Tina for Queen," says Francine Hunter; according to her, she was too busy organizing shows and parties to worry about becoming royalty. In fact, Hunter feels she was partly responsible for the Mudd's initial success. "My twenty-eighth birthday on January 18, 1978, was the first real party at the Mudd. Before that it was a very local bar which no one outside the neighborhood knew about. I invited all the radio and record company people I knew along with all the underground artists and filmmakers. After that, it became this happening spot." Hunter also takes credit for presenting fashion in a theater piece for the first time since the 1939 Hollywood movie *The Women*. Her Mudd extravaganza, *Night School*, was a multimedia eight-act play chronicling all the varieties of schools from convent to beauty to obedience. It was an educational experience, the kind of zany ground-breaking event Mudd did so well.

Other nights, you could get a massage courtesy of *Wet* magazine, hear Marilyn (a female performer, not the British singer of the eighties) sing undeniable truths like "Sex Means Nothing when You're Dead," even mourn the death of disco at a not-so-mock funeral. Or just stand around with a slight sneer and exude attitude until you were appointed upper-echelon Mudd royalty yourself.

D.j. Anita Sarko remembers the achievements that led to her own unauthorized Mudd royalty status. A former law student who wore sunglasses to class so she could sleep, Sarko was more alert about the career possibilities inherent in the club scene. "I was a radio d.j. in Atlanta. First, I worked at a college station where their idea of progressive music was Boz Scaggs. So, I'd play these independent singles and imports from my own collection. The musical director, of course, heard the shows and knew he hadn't programed those records." Soon, he wasn't programing Anita either.

From there she wound up on a Top 40 station for a brief stint and then came to New York where her friends the B-52's told her about the Mudd. "The doormen wouldn't let me in because I wasn't cool enough, so I snuck in one night. I heard the music and thought, 'Wait a minute, this is what they're playing? They only have two songs.' The d.j.'s taste was a little wanting. He played very Brooklyn-Bronx, Max's Kansas City rock and roll. I knew I could do better."

So, like a new wave Ruby Keeler, she spun her way into Mass's heart and ultimately landed the d.j.'s job, bringing her own chutzpah and record collection to it. "I like to be a reactionary. I love to throw in an element that'll absolutely antagonize the crowd. Everyone used to walk out when I played African music, but Steve said, 'It's cool. I love it.' Tina Weymouth of the Talking Heads sent me a note saying, 'I understand what you're doing. Keep it up.' I just had fun with music." Now, people are much more braced for the aurally unpredictable; they almost expect a Puccini aria after a tribal chant.

"Working with Mass," Sarko says, "was like boot camp. The regulars were performers in the Mudd Club drama—they all had their roles, and he was Dr. Mudd. It was conceptual art as life. The door policy was Steve saying, 'I don't want any plaid shirts tonight' or 'No fatsos on weekends. They displace the thin ones.' People thought they were cool if they got in, and what did they get into? A dump.

"Steve would say, 'Why didn't you do this, why don't you do that?' He was trying to make me adapt to New York. I was a real hayseed and he made me shape up." But after having drinks and ashtrays thrown at her and being "bullied" by Mass, Sarko decided she was only being shaped up to be knocked down and she quit. Mass lured her back by building a see-through Plexiglas d.j. booth so people couldn't hit her, but a month later she quit again. Currently, she reigns as the music programmer at Palladium's Mike Todd Room.

Robert Molnar, a prominent downtown designer, learned about fashion—or coats anyway—as a Mudd coatcheck. "Steve told me I had to turn in my tips, and I was so naive I did. I didn't catch on for a whole year." Later Molnar was made a doorman—a dubious promotion—and remembers, "I'd have to run out in the snow and give poker chips to the people who could get in. Some nights Steve would say to me 'Don't let anyone in for free tonight.' I'd say, 'But Steve, you told me you want artists and musicians.' 'I don't care—no one for free,' he'd answer. I remember one night I threw Keith Haring out." So much for Mass starting the concept of a downtown elite. Let's say at least two nights a week he did.

Mass explains his own door policy in retrospect, saying, "If someone had taken the trouble to create a look, that was great. But anybody could hire a limo for twenty-five dollars an hour. I already knew the downtown luminaries of the art world like Tony Shafrazi, and I also knew people in the literary scene. I knew who William S. Burroughs was, whereas if he'd walked up to Xenon in 1979, they'd probably have had no idea who he was. I fancied myself a Mad Hatter at a surrealistic breakfast table—all these people telling me their credentials and me putting the king in the back, the queen on the right, and the toilet attendant up front. Old hippies weren't allowed in. Of course, Allen Ginsberg read his work here . . . so, we broke our own rules."

Says Molnar, "He was nuts, but he was brilliant. He had it all planned out." What Mass didn't plan out, though, was his conviction on an income-tax-related charge (a similar charge to the one Studio 54's Steve Rubell and Ian Schrager faced in 1980) and the creative people's eventual desertion of the Mudd, which he sold in 1982.

But downtown culture didn't fall into the mud with the Mudd. The foundation had been built—a whole legion of creative artists and revelers not willing to lead any lifestyle but the off-the-beaten-track one. Their culture was not dependent on any one place as long as there was some place they could go to strut their stuff. So, clubs catering to downtown contined to open with more and more frequency, and even though many of them became fleeting memories before the second-night invitations arrived, the overall diversity and choice grew as the downtown style became more appealing to larger numbers of people.

Howard Stein and Pepo Vanini of Xenon disco fame opened the Rock Lounge, a two-level rock club that tried but failed to capture downtown's imagination. "I'd sit there and cry," says Anita Sarko, who worked there as a d.j. and booking agent after her Mudd stint ended. "Pepo's attitude was, 'I don't approve of these people, but I'll give you money to do something.' But there wasn't enough money to do it right." And the attitude was definitely wrong.

In October of 1979, on the same day the hostages were taken in Iran, Rudolf Pieper and Jim Fouratt opened Pravda, the only one-night club in New York's history, sort of the *Moose Murders* of nightlife, but better. "Steve Mass was paranoid of a club opening next to him catering to a similar clientele and being a better club," says Rudolf. But he's the one who should have been paranoid since Pravda didn't have a certificate of occupancy from the city's buildings department. "And the neighborhood felt SoHo should remain untouched by anything artistic. Little did they know what was to come." Brief as it was, Pravda was prophetic in its mix of video, art, music, fashion (a Betsey Johnson show) and avant-garde people. Of course, most clubs last longer—about six months.

Rudolf, who's from Germany via Argentina, or vice versa, won European society points in 1969 for opening the first big hippie nightclub in Berlin. "It was open twenty-four hours a day, seven days a week. People lived there. The d.j. would play birdcalls for hours and people would dance to them." After a stint in Brazil (going to other people's clubs), Rudolf teamed with notorious tastemaker Jim Fouratt, something Francine Hunter also takes credit for ("I was Rudolf's girlfriend at the time and was one of the people who encouraged him to work with Jim"). It turns out it's not the kind of thing anyone would want to brag about. The association ended in 1982 with Fouratt landing a $17-million suit against Rudolf, which neither will discuss now for fear of endangering the jackpot.

Says Rudolf, "Jim was working at Hurrah's the first successful rock disco. He had one of his famous tantrums and scandals with the people there and was fired. Observing that, I hired him to book Pravda." Fouratt claims he "left" Hurrah's after the owners unfairly chopped down the artists' door percentages, but until that point, he'd transformed the club into "the prototype for rock discos across the country." Love him or leave him, Fouratt did try to give nightlife some substance to back up the attitude.

When Pravda didn't work out, Jim and Rudolf (calling themselves Average Normal, Inc.) nailed a sleazoid location on West 39th Street and turned it into Danceteria, a club that dazzled downtown with its frenzied energy and steady stream of local and out-of-town bands that were clearly the best of the weirdest, the most entertaining of the worst and just the best. The club was an instant success. But when they turned away a Democratic party fete for Jimmy Carter, claiming there was already another bash booked there on that day, it was really because they were afraid the event would lead to an investigation. Danceteria was lacking a few essential licenses. After eight months of fun, the club caved in to the law. Jim and Rudolf pulled up to the front door one night to find that twenty of their employees were being held at the local precinct—charged with illegally selling alcohol.

"I knew it was a time bomb set to go off," says the club's doorman, Haoui Montaug, in retrospect. "It was illegal. We were posing as a private club—except when you put ads in the *Village Voice*, it's hard to justify that."

After setting up shop everywhere from the Peppermint Lounge to Blitz in West Hempstead, Long Island, the duo opened a new Danceteria on February 2, 1982, on the site of a failing club called Interferon. It even topped the old Danceteria in that it had three floors (and ultimately a fourth floor, Congo Bill's, and a rooftop, Wuthering Heights) done in a kitsch fifties/futuristic style the Jetsons and the Kramdens both would have felt at home in. The new club featured a multitude of d.j.'s, video monitors, lounges, performance spaces and everything but a sex clinic and popcorn concession. Danceteria's slogan is "The supermarket of style," which is why it's still alive today; supermarkets last longer than clubs. But shopping at Danceteria makes for a refreshingly unpretentious if sometimes all-too-real slice of life à la mode.

"The 'A' crowd never went to Danceteria by their own will," says Rudolf. "I've never had big celebrities and Studio 54 types coming regularly. They never really felt comfortable here because it's not a club for people who want status confirmed. I challenged the status of the established people. Danceteria people want a certain kind of anarchism, a little edge of raunchiness.

"I can't say, 'Dino de Laurentiis comes here,' but I don't want these people if I have to sit at their table and be nice to them." Rudolf, a true German (or Argentinian) gentleman, would sit at their table and be nice to them anyway. His anarchy is extremely refined.

His philosophy of nightlife, by the way, is "Most advanced, yet acceptable." That sums up all of downtown after midnight, which is always one step beyond, but still something your mother could love. It's mass culture given the twist of eccentricity and the sparkle of elitism. Appalling, yet somehow adorable.

Since Danceteria, other clubs have opened faster than you can say, "Hey bud, let's party," and each one has had something out of the ordinary to recommend it. Berlin and the Continental were funky, atmospheric clubs that didn't start happening until around three in the morning, but their doors slammed shut when the roof was blown off the afterhours racket in early 1983. According to the *New York Times* of February 22, 1983, "For more than two years, agents of the Federal Bureau of Investigation ran an undercover operation in the Continental and another downtown afterhours club in Manhattan, an operation that led them through a maze of possible payoffs to police officers, stolen goods, evidence of a counterfeiting ring, and finally, murder." Now that's downtown action.

The article also asserted that underneath the evening clothes of Arthur Weinstein, Continental's co-owner, "was a transmitter that allowed the FBI to monitor every word he said." Weinstein countered in Stephen Saban's *Details* magazine column that he only wore a wire once. In any case, the very weekend after the *Times*' article, all the illegal afterhours clubs prematurely saw the afterlife. They were a memory.

Before the crackdown, an afterhours club called AM-PM had developed a passionate following despite—or maybe because of—the place's aggressive, almost sleazy intensity. "It's amazing the mixture of people I met there," says Fred Rothbell-Mista, a former film editor who made his entree into the nightlife world working at AM-PM and went on to handling VIP's at the Limelight. "You could get high—on pot, or whatever—and you didn't have to go home. And it was glamorous. We were all kids discovering staying-up-late for the first time." Among the "kids" were people such as Robert De Niro, David Bowie, Grace Jones and John Belushi (who reportedly stopped to party there on his way to ruin) mixing with a slew of unknowns with spiked hair, and spiked drinks. For AM-PM's closing, host Vito Bruno organized—What else?—a funeral party. "The finest Italian florist did a fabulous Gates of Heaven display," he says, remembering the tearful event. But for some, the memory of AM-PM lies somewhere south of that.

Only Bruno could turn a "funeral" into a party. And it was far from his last fete—he resurfaced at Roxy: a roller disco during the week, which was transformed into a sizzling swirl of hip-hop culture mixed with downtown chic on weekends. The Roxy, it seemed, attracted everyone's attention. People with names like Muffy, Buffy and Baird boogied next to leather-jacketed Third World spray-can Gauguins, and they never acted as if they were Margaret Mead on an anthropological expedition. They really mixed, and the super hip, super hip-hop scratch noise of guest d.j.'s like Afrika Bambaataa helped keep all the pieces of the jigsaw in place.

Now, clubs are more segregated and less spontaneous affairs. Club owners don't just dazzle downtown, they *plan* to dazzle it in as many ways they can think of. More recent clubs aren't just hangouts, they're P.T. Barnum-style gimmicks executed on a grandiose scale. There's been Kamikaze, an art bar; Pizza-A-Go-Go, a pizzeria/dance club; Limelight, a church-turned-disco; Area, an ever-changing theme museum; Private Eyes, a video club studded with thirty-four screens (and sometimes as many people); and Palladium, the biggest multimedia experience of them all.

If there's been any trend in downtown nightlife in the last five years, it's that clubs have gotten bigger and downtowners can lose the people they come in with more easily than ever. As the downtown population—and the population that wants to drool over it—grows, clubs expand in size and spirit in a never-ending "Can you top this?" competition. Can they top the simple joys of the Mudd Club? Probably not, but the constant changes of decor will help people forget to compare.

"All the flux makes me feel like I want to keep changing as well," says Haoui Montaug, who's worked the door at at least twelve clubs in fifteen years of living it up and never living it down. "I like change. The only interesting part of nightlife is the newness of it."

As he said that, new clubs became old, old ones became new again, and the familiar routine of going out and bopping-till-you-drop became fresh for the millionth time. Somehow, getting clubbed to death is still something worth staying out late for.

3

East of Eden, North of SoHo »

This mural is in a museum—the street museum of the East Village, where there's art everywhere you look and even in some places you don't look.

We've already said that downtown is no longer a location, it's a state of mind. But let's face it—that state of mind began and happens to exist mostly . . . downtown.

Walk down St. Marks Place and you're on the Champs Elysées of life below 14th Street. Local kids in ill-fitting overcoats covering purposely mismatched outfits peer through their fifties nerd glasses (without lenses—a fashion, not vision, statement). If they could see, they'd notice a procession of glamor ghouls wearing black from head to toe and wielding Madonna-inspired crosses to ward off vampires (and Madonna). No one even notices the handful of punk survivors standing around wondering what happened to their movement. Though thinking about that makes those survivors angry and keeps them punk for a while longer.

Punk or not, the East Villagers are so emaciated—either from bulimia, fashion consciousness or malnutrition—that the only way they can gain weight is to cut themselves and hope a scab will form. They follow the Edie Sedgwick diet—drugs and occasional free buffets—until they look like severe and gorgeous wire hangers. Then they shop around furiously looking for cheap long-sleeved items to hang on themselves. You'll find them, and everything else, in the East Village. Vintage clothing shops like Trash and Vaudeville and Andy's Chee-Pees sell some of the most expensive cheap clothing in New York, while newer boutiques sell cheap expensive clothing. St. Marks Bookshop offers every esoteric book imaginable for those who don't necessarily believe that *Hollywood Wives* is a seminal twentieth-century work. Records are bought and sold at Sounds, where over the music you hear the comforting drone of bartering, but you can't bargain for a falafel next door: it's a prix fixe, tahini sauce (but not gratuity) included. Sushi joints litter the street—Japan's revenge for losing the war, some say—but a slice of pizza with extra cheese is more to the local taste. At Gem Spa on the corner, you can spend your daily $2 luxury allowance on a morning cup of coffee and the monthly paper (*East Village Eye*). Morning, by the way, is about one in the afternoon.

At night all the downtowners swarm the streets with the incredibly natural glow that only comes from doing very hard drugs. Neatly coiffed gays file into Boybar, where they cruise their own reflections and go home alone (they're afraid of that new disease—personal interaction), but the reflections are generally attractive. Boybar emphasizes a much more aesthetic and imaginative image than the down-and-dirty bars further west, where there *are* no mirrors.

Not that St. Marks Place is totally pristine: it's only half pristine, the other half you wouldn't want to test with a white glove. Ironically, though, it's the slightly ragged half the neighborhood is fighting for, because that's the "authentic" half. The rest is the result of outsiders coming in with aerosol cans and making it all lilac-scented and lovely. To most of the real East Villagers, just the words "lilac-scented and lovely" are enough to warrant a barf bag.

But that hasn't stopped the well-fed middle-class professionals from swarming into this last residential horizon, the Shangri-la-de-da of commercial exhilaration. The lack of available rental housing in New York has forced tens of thousands of them to invade previously déclassé areas, revamping them into places where a yuppie might get inspired, not mugged. It happened to East LA and the East End of London. In New York it happened to Park Slope, Chelsea and Columbus Avenue; in the mid-to-late 1970s, it happened to SoHo, which went from a decaying manufacturing area to a spruced-up, expensive culture-vulture haven that teems with tourists on the weekend. Now, the East Village is going through a similar transition, and residents are simultaneously thrilled to see their neighborhood becoming more livable and appalled to find a lot of the character moving out along with the rubble.

The East Village is technically the area between 14th Street and Houston, bounded by the Bowery and the East River. A melting pot for immigrants for 150 years, it's now a melting pot for real estate dealers like Harry Helmsley who are closing in with $ signs in their eyes. The neighborhood's become so profitable that one dilapidated sixteen-story building on Avenue B—the Christodora—was recently sold for a 2000% profit. When *New York Magazine* subtitled their Lower East Side cover story "There goes the neighborhood," they weren't kidding. But a whole new neighborhood was coming in.

"I went away in the summer of 1984," says Brian Butterick, one of the managers of the Pyramid Club (which is on Avenue A), "and when I came back, this glamorous LA-type sushi bar had opened next door. It's inevitable, and sad, but we did have a part in it," he laughs, "and at least we can make some money off it."

Not everyone is so lucky. After twenty-seven years of serving pizza and pirogen, the Orchidia Italian/Ukrainian Restaurant was forced to close when the landlord jacked up the rent more than 400%. Theater for the New City, which along with La Mama presents dozens of experimental new plays every year, was considering a move in the face of a rent increase of approximately 500%. The St. Marks Cinema, a neighborhood landmark which offered a recent double bill and tons of cinematic atmosphere for $4, turned into a shopping center right out of *Day of the Dead*—formerly one of its most popular midnight attractions. And Manic Panic, a popular St. Marks boutique, went thataway after eight years of selling clothing, wigs and accessories so eye-catching many of the ideas were picked up by Seventh Avenue (which didn't give credit, of course). Their rent would have at least quadrupled, forcing sisters Tish and Snooky Bellomo to close up shop and pursue their long-stifled show biz dreams instead. "People with commercial space should have some kind of protection," says Tish. "I'd suggest people think twice before building up a business here because somebody else always moves in."

The East Village, she adds, "was hot in the sixties with the Fillmore East and the Electric Circus. But when that trend faded out, it went back into a slum. Now it's very mixed. You get yuppies walking next to bums and junkies. It still doesn't know what it wants to be because they can't get rid of the bums that quickly."

"You used to hear eight different kinds of music and smell different kinds of ethnic smells on the street," says musician Elliott Sharp, who has his own avant-garde record label, Zoar. "But that's all disappearing."

"You used to know everyone on your block," echoes magazine editor/fashion stylist Mary Kaye Schilling, as if part of an anti-gentrification Greek chorus. "You still do, but you don't necessarily want to."

The touristy transformation of the neighborhood into an artsy-fartsy Coney Island is undeniable. But what all the people shedding crocodile tears over the good old days forget is that in the good old days you couldn't even enter Tompkins Square Park unless you were a world-class runner, and Alphabetland was a no-man's-land of burnt-out buildings and bodegas that bustled with creative energy only because you *had* to be creative to survive in such a slum center. Now, some of the locals who fought with their landlords for years over bathroom facilities have actually gotten to take a bath. The rubble is still ominously visible—the city, which owns many of the di-

- The East Village is an eclectic swirl of boutiques, promotional posters, fashion statements and "For Sale" signs. Immensely adding to the local color is rapper Dean Johnson, whose clean-shaved head glistens almost as brightly as the bewigged domes of Manic Panic's co-owner Snooky Bellomo (*right*) and one of her workers. Hanging out amidst the bustle of St. Marks Place, Bellomo might have reason for manic panic—the store's succumbed to gentrification.

lapidated buildings, is waiting for optimum prices before cleaning them up. But in between the garbage heaps are new, funky boutiques and galleries that have redefined the neighborhood with their idiosyncratic and comfortable ambience and affordable chic. These small, offbeat, living room-style spots are a far cry from their larger, more sterile SoHo equivalents, where a graffiti board with crayons in the back seems so calculated it must have been drawn up by an interior designer. Not surprisingly, just as SoHo once thumbed its nose at the uptown establishment, a lot of the East Village's appeal stems from its disdain of SoHo, which it feels has been about as avant-garde as Times Square since the late seventies.

The East Villagers say their neighborhood is more spontaneous, more combustible, and as much as some residents may complain, still pulsing with a twenty-four-hour creative vitality that makes it throb. The complaints are only because the youthquake of the sixties is registering on the seismograph again, and downtowners are afraid that too much commercialization of it might turn the tremors into arthritic pains.

Here you can buy dresses for men, cowboy boots for women and books on outer-body experiences—or the experiences themselves. You can pick up that *Julia* lunchbox you lost as a kid, that Twister game you bring out when you want the guests to leave and that adorable retro, and adorably useful, TV tray you pull out afterwards. Here when someone says, "Why don't you come up and see my etchings," he really means it.

The neighborhood is becoming such a living monument to art that one artist who pogoed to his own opening in a giant spring was stopped by police only because he was going against traffic. (Since a lot of tougher street crime was cleaned up, this type of thing now qualifies as a major East Village police problem.) Even ordinary household items are being treated as art. When Mary Kaye Schilling went to buy a bouquet of flowers at a local florist, the outraged Rastafarian owner stopped her from assembling daisies and roses into the assortment she wanted. "Hey, that's art," he instructed, "and must be sold exactly as it's arranged." She didn't want art, she wanted flowers.

She should have gone to the Life Cafe, where you can't get flowers, but at least you get a sympathetic atmosphere and guacamole. The place is the hub of Alphabetland activity, the Russian Tea Room of a scene that's never heard of the RTR. "There was nothing here when we arrived," remembers Kathy Kirkpatrick, who, along with her ex-husband David, started the Life on Avenue B in 1981. "We always liked living on the edge, and this was certainly the edge. But we also saw the charm that was hidden here." The comfortable, pretension-free hangout quickly became a home for all the local artists who were tired of studying the alien creatures crawling around their apartments and preferred to study each other over a bowl of chili.

The restaurant's growth helped Alphabetland to develop a bit along with it. "When we took it over, this space was a storefront no one would touch," says Kathy. "A total disaster, as bad as any of the abandoned buildings around here." Braced for a challenge, the Lifes, as their friends call them, turned the space into an antique furniture shop whose menu catered strictly to coffee achievers—coffee was the only item on it. But as starving canvas achievers filled the place and needed something more substantial to digest, the place burgeoned into a full-fledged restaurant with *Life* magazine covers masking the cracks in the walls and Mexican concoctions filling the cracks in the menu. Cracked people usually filled the tables.

Because of its local importance, the Life Cafe is one of the few commercial spots to face compassion instead of gentrification. "Our original landlord," says Kathy, "recognized that we're the cornerstone of activity in the neighborhood—Sur Rodney (Sur) of Gracie Mansion Gallery said, 'The survival of Life Cafe is crucial to the survival of galleries on the Lower East Side.' So, when he wanted to sell to a new landlord who's from the Upper East Side and didn't know us from Adam, we held an art auction at a club, 8 B.C., to 'pay off' the old landlord so he wouldn't transfer the collection rights." The Life held onto its life.

And now, rather than being in the middle of a hellhole, it's in the middle of the most upgraded New York neighborhood in recent memory. "I remember when there was a shooting gallery across from us," says Kathy, referring not to people getting shot (not uncommon either), but to people shooting up. "We'd watch people wait on line for it to open up so they could go in and do their business, then stagger out. It was really sickening.

"Now it's safe. In February 1984 a huge concentration of police called Operation Pressure Point cracked down on the drug traffic and had a tremendous effect on the area. It's prettier to look at a real neighborhood and not see people drooling in the streets." And the few people who *are* still drooling are probably just performance artists honing their craft.

Beauregard Houston-Montgomery, a writer for *Details* and the *East Village Eye*, began renting his St. Marks Place apartment in 1975 but didn't move in for a whole year because the place needed so much work. "And after I moved in, I'd have to go to Beverly Hills in the winter because there was no heat or hot water." Most people in his situation would have stayed in the Hills, but Beauregard had the pioneering spirit, something that usually dissolves the minute you slide into a hot tub or eat an American croissant. "The East Village was a challenge because it was literally unlivable," he says. "You couldn't even get near any of the stores because the streets were all ripped up. I approached it like Eva Gabor in 'Green Acres,' creating my apartment out of my own imagination and very few dollars and turning it into a shrine to snowdomes and kitsch art. *Casa Vogue* photographed it in 1982, and the pictures are still considered too radical to use. They're in their files, though, and the editors still talk about it at meetings."

Beauregard's apartment rented for a mere $100 a month then, but now, he says aptly, "They could get seven fifty for the closet in the hallway." Now, as the neighborhood becomes upgraded, he's more like another Gabor—Zsa Zsa—in *Queen of Outer Space*, feeling more and more alien in his own environs. "You can't walk down the street without being knocked over by baby carriages. These people aren't artists, they're computer executives. They look at you like you're weird. I helped create the neighborhood, and now I feel punished for it when I see the tour bus pull up or when I can't leave the house because they're filming an MTV video on the stoop." What Beauregard doesn't say is that he *does* look weird—his petticoats would have sent Dolley Madison into a spin—but not nearly as weird as the tourists who revel in the East Village as if it were some sort of walk-through Ripley's "Believe It or Not."

Fortunately for them, there's a lot to revel in. Wander a few blocks west to Astor Place and you'll bump into a crowd of people waiting for emergency coiffure help. This is Astor Place Hair Designers, a palace of total ego gratification—it's quick and cheap, the haircuts are usually at least workmanlike, and, when you exit, the entire line of future customers bursts into wild applause over your new do.

Parade it around in an impromptu outdoor fashion show and if you see an interesting piece of used clothing some street vendor is hawking, add that to your new look. But add it quickly—the vendors evaporate the second the police show up. And if you're interested in a porno magazine like, let's say *Bodacious Ta-Ta's*, you'd better grab it even quicker than that because the police will almost certainly want it for themselves.

Sport your new look (or *Ta-Ta's*) down a few blocks to Tower Records, possibly the biggest record store in the world, a high-tech vinyl museum that carries about seventy thousand titles. If you don't find something you like here, you're tone-deaf.

> • **Alphabetland—Avenues A through D— not only has life, it has the Life Cafe, an enduring meeting ground for local artists, musicians and those hungry for guacamole. Pretension is not on the menu.**

Back to the heart of the East Village, on Second Avenue, nibble on a greasy kielbasa and slurp in the borscht, which is sometimes cold even when it's not supposed to be, at Veselka or Kiev, or, for more hoity-toity moods, try some curried apple-walnut-raisin-cucumber something-or-other that passes for the soup of the day at 103 Second Avenue. Fortunately, the food doesn't matter much here. It's a public showroom—a place to see and be seen—and it's open all night. Later, wonder why everyone looks like unhappy rabbits, a line from *All About Eve*, when that camp classic invariably plays with *Sunset Boulevard* at Theatre Eighty St. Marks, the city's most—and least—Hollywood-style revival house. It's basically a dump, but the stars' photos in the lobby ("Mommie dearest" eyes you on the way in) and overall Tinseltown stench give this place an aura of bizarre fabulousness.

That's where sensible people would have stopped their tour a couple of years ago, but by now, Alphabetland is so alive with galleries, shops and clubs, it requires less courage than Courreges. No longer is it the eerie, smoke-filled, MTV-style sleazehole portrayed in the movie *Alphabet City* (though that element hasn't been totally whited-out yet). Now, it's so art-conscious that even the streets and buildings are covered with it. "There's Buzzards In The Bushes, They're Fighting Over Worms" proclaims one cryptic street mural, and those who aren't in on the symbolism walk by in brisk terror. Everyone else enjoys the area's off-kilter but exciting balance between the chi-chi and the inescapably real.

The balance will keep changing, whether people want it to or not. And the only reason some might not want it to change, according to one landlord, is "They don't own buildings like I do."

"The changes are inevitable," says Timothy Greenfield-Sanders, a photographer who put some of his earnings into East Village real estate in 1974 and is now reaping the benefit of it (one of his buildings contains two successful galleries, Civilian Warfare and Semaphore East). "I've lived through addicts throwing syringes in the street in front of my kids. There's no comparison now."

As for all the small, independent businesses that are being forced to shut down, he says, "Please! The Baltyk Restaurant had one good dish—the soup—and the rest of the food was greasy garbage. Besides, they had over twenty good years here. You can't force neighborhoods to stay the same. And there are plenty of greasy spoons left."

Amazingly, a lot of people insist they want all the "greasy garbage" back, just the way it was. They'd gotten used to it. They lived it, loved it, became part of it. "I liked the neighborhood better when it was messy," says Bobby Bradley, who originated the Pyramid Club, then was kicked out of the partnership in 1984. "Five years ago it was a paradise here. It's a good thing they cleaned out the junkies, but they only did it to pave the way for real estate increases. Given a choice between cheap rent and junkies or high rent, business suits and a spic-and-span life, I'd have to go with the junkies." Too bad the junkies wanted no part of you unless you were willing to make a contribution.

Maybe what disturbs the die-hard East Villagers is that control over their neighborhood is being taken out of their hands—no one likes it when his own personal discovery becomes noticed and adopted by others—or maybe they really are concerned about their creative surroundings. In either case, they're definitely disturbed.

"The future of the neighborhood frightens me so much that I don't think about it anymore," says Beauregard. "Incredibly enough, there are still some esoteric things left here. Hopefully, it's not going to turn into Columbus Avenue. If it does, I'll have to move." His rent has miraculously gone up to a mere $138 a month—staying in the same apartment for years is the best revenge—but he says, "I live in constant subliminal paranoia. I'm very lucky I'm not a poor person who can't afford a lawyer."

"I hate what's happening in this neighborhood," says Victor Weaver, editor of *S.T.H. (Straight to Hell), The Manhattan Review of Unnatural Acts*, a letters-to-the-editor gay porn magazine that's been feted and glorified in downtown clubs. "Getting mugged last weekend was almost reassuring that this area isn't improving too fast."

❰❰ ow Rent, High Society ❱❱

For nightclub diva and aspiring superstar Sally Randall, the hat isn't just the icing on the cake, it's the focal point of the outfit. Benjamin Van De Seijp and dancer Patrick DiaGiovanni agree.

How, besides taking the Second Avenue bus down to St. Marks Place, does one arrive at a downtown sensibility?

Four out of five doctors would agree that in most cases downtown specimens either come from faraway alien cultures (i.e. small towns), from insipid middle-class families right in New York and its suburbs or from the most upscale sections of Mars. What sends them to the creative fringes of Manhattan? Their parents, who were fed up with behavior that was definitely not going to impress the Joneses. Or their own creative will nearly deadened by the routine of a contented domestic life—the American dream—a life so predictably coffee-klatschy that if a toilet backs up it's an exciting day. How much opportunity do budding designers or musicians have to express their creative urges in a home where they're being counted on to take the preprofessional route whether they want to or not (and to fix the toilet in the meantime)? Not much, especially when it sinks in that preprofessional usually leads to professional, which often leads to an ulcer.

"Even now that I'm a fairly successful designer," says one very successful designer, "my mother says I should get a part-time job just for security's sake."

A horrifying thought—imagine running out of your own glittering fashion show to pack bags at the A & P? But leave your phone machine on permanent "Record" and you've cut off all parental disapproval for the last time. That kind of pressure doesn't exist here, where the more unorthodox you are, the higher echelon you assume in the pantheon of anti-celebrities. The more daringly you throw fabrics together, make your hair go against its natural shape or defy traditional concepts of beauty, the more quickly you'll be ushered into club VIP rooms with open bars. No one of any social standing actually pays for drinks.

Downtown you can make your own rules, and to hell with what the folks back home think of them. As for "security's sake," that's hardly what one comes here for. In fact, the second anything gets too secure, it gets boring, a reality that forces downtown personalities and establishments to continually keep up an edge of disorder and a sense that anything still might happen: fighting off the rigor mortis of complacent success. And anyone rebelling against the stability of a dreary upbringing thrives on the evanescent thrill of new places and the sense that if you're not dropping the right names, you could be dropped out of society with a resounding thud. It's a diverting game, especially if you can trump everyone else's pretenses and win. You've got to — because bubbling beneath all the creative innovations, downtown is just as plagued by snobbery, trend following and one-upmanship as the middle-class world it takes off from. It's a hierarchical society in itself, with pretenders, hangers-on and bloodsuckers matching the true creative people every step of the way.

It also has a deceptive security, even for the people who claim to hate security. Just like in high school where there were always a few seniors who seemed to enjoy being left back, there are plenty who prefer comforting stagnation to taking a chance on movement, whether it's forward or not. Others want to get left back, not because it represents a safe step, but because the crass and commercial uptown world couldn't possibly understand their fabulousness. Below 23rd Street, their work reaps money, notoriety and fulfillment. To water it down and risk that nosebleed would leave a bad taste in their sewing machines.

More likely, though, downtowners are more than willing to hone their ideas "down" and enjoy a creative freedom you can't find anywhere else— while preparing to go "up" to the big time. And there's less and less dilution necessary as designers and artists start downtown, then saturate Middle America with all their inventiveness intact. Uptown craves downtown for what it is—outrageous and different.

"I don't want to do the normal stuff. There's enough of that," said Stephen Sprouse, a designer of Sixties and street-inspired fashion who made a big splash before drowning in bankruptcy. His was the quintessential downtown success story—colorful, meteoric and totally trendsetting. It was also totally short. "Sometimes I think my success is funny," said the then-prosperous designer—a quiet, unassuming guy who seemed cryptically bemused by it all. "I just do what I like."

Once ensconced in the downtown world, the trick is to chew up all you were spoon-fed by American mass culture and spit it out in the form of bitingly satirical art, laced with overkill. It should both blow mass culture to smithereens and make it the object of cult worship. Those in the punk movement took a more one-sided approach. They tried to totally annihilate the establishment—but that grew boring, and they had to annihilate themselves as a final performance piece. Now, everyone's extra careful to never grow boring.

So, instead of making solid-color conventional clothing, designer/boutique owner Jo Dean assembles outfits out of dozens of tiny pieces of material, everything from chenille bedspreads to lace doilies, which she fuses into a sort of glorified ragamuffin look. "People wear them to parties—to be seen—and in cars—to not be seen," says Dean, who moved her store from 51st Street and Ninth Avenue to St. Marks Place and found the step down was actually a giant step up. And at a makeshift living-room-turned-performance-space called Chandalier, where the sign outside says, "Turn knob, first landing," the Alien Comic (Tom Murrin) unleashes a barrage of absurdly funny observations, all of which he somehow makes relate to his endless array of impromptu props and headdresses, which are picked out of inspiration and out of garbage cans. He never repeats his material, and though his shows are only fifteen minutes long, if you went home and played them in slow motion, you'd get a lifetime full of wit and wisdom to live by. He is never boring.

For downtown, "boring" is a dirty word. "Demented," "outrageous" and "absurd" can be good words. Dressing the part is crucial. But there's something more important than looking good, and that's making it so big it doesn't matter what you look like—and then still looking good just to prove you can do it even when you don't have to. Everyone's on creative overdrive, and even the successful ones are constantly pushing forward, because the slightest stagnation could find them buried in the next wave. Stores try to jump on new trends before their rivals have even got wind of them, and art dealers follow their own heat-seeking missiles in a perpetual star search. Clubs outvarnish each other in attempts to be fresh, desperately realizing that the second a better, or just newer, club opens, they become yesterday's news. And, of course, it's better not to have been news at all than to be yesterday's news.

Forearmed with such wisdom, the kids of downtown launch their creative quests at a disarmingly young age. Some at nineteen look like they've partied and explored so much that a little Porcelana wrinkle cream might be in order. Fortunately, a lot of them have the concomitant smarts and business acumen to make it in their chosen field. Ignoring the traditional college and job-hunting routes, they learn at the proverbial school of hard knocks, shoving their way into clubs, hawking their wares to buyers and generally immersing themselves in the concrete jungle-gym at which anyone can play. They emerge with drink tickets instead of diplomas and move on to better parties instead of grad school. Most consider it a useful and inexpensive education. The ones who get caught up in the notoriety they get as after-midnight freaks-of-the-hour forget to plan ahead, but the smart ones segue smoothly from nightlife into real life.

Some of them do nothing but dress up so they'll look good as they dream of overnight stardom and collect on their trust funds. Some of them don't

> • Designer and "Queen of the Night" Dianne Brill with club entrepreneur Rudolf in happier times together (now he's seen in other designer's clothes). Both are major forces on a scene that craves their invaluable names on invitations.

even do that much. But all of them are so socially adept that something substantial often comes out of their party skills.

People laughed at James St. James (his name for the week), a nineteen-year-old trust-fund darling who wears feather boas and carries Flintstones' lunchboxes filled with little wooden Fisher-Price people that he puts in little scooters as he vrooms around the room with all the rambunctiousness of youth. But James is the one *Newsweek* picked up on in their 1985 story on afterhours society as an example of New York style. James is the one "Mayflower Madam" Sidney Biddle Barrows shared fashion tips with, Drew Barrymore asked to go on a shopping spree with and rock singer Marc Almond talked turkey with—all in one breathless night. It wasn't that surprising when James was suddenly in demand for styling jobs and TV appearances. Even the people who thought he was kind of a joke had a sneaky feeling he couldn't help parlaying all that attention into something worthy of it.

As much as it may fill the old set with jealous distaste, the new set like James—an average boy-next-door type who transformed himself overnight into a downtown flashheap—a wallet photo of his hair-parted-down-the-middle former self his only tie to the old days—may well be the future of New York style. The new kids on the block are tireless style mavens who both amaze their elders and leave them wondering why *they* were only collating papers at that age before advancing to a very prestigious career in de-collating.

Feisty Andy Anderson, a Missouri-born-hick–turned–club-kingpin has already been through more fashion looks than Cher. What's more, he's a veteran of club bookings, having modeled Amadeus-suggested clothes for an East Village store called La Coppia at Pizza-A-Go-Go, organized a paper fashion show at Limelight and produced Danceteria's low-rent versions of "The Gong Show" and "Puttin' on the Hits" among dozens of other events. For his "Gong Show," Anderson moderated a wonderfully dire and tasteless procession of acts, which ranged from *Crimes-of-Passion* readings to just plain crimes of passion. ("Heterosexuality is a sick and boring lifestyle," said one judge, gonging two straight men indulging in repressed athletic dancing.) For "Puttin' on the Hits," a takeoff on the TV lip-sync extravaganza, Anderson cheerily introduced each mock Tina Turner, Sade and Bette Midler with understandable excitement. Most of the contestants were better than the ones on the actual show. A pregnant Madonna lookalike singing "Like a Virgin" was inspired, but the judges were more impressed with a drag queen doing "My Funny Valentine" a la Nico, the cult songstress who performed in the Velvet Underground. She was by far the most esoteric entry all-around, and her perfect score for originality was well deserved—the mortified crowd had never even heard of Nico. When this dubious diva was announced as the winner, Anderson had to use his considerable wiles to keep the crowd from lynching the panel of judges. These people won't take any shit.

Other kids on the scene are already so accomplished, they could already lip sync to their own records. Bartender-turned-Mister-Show-Biz David Ilku shows up everywhere in enough guises to make Lon Chaney look limited. Young designer Michael Schmidt, the touchie-feelie demigod of skinny chic, shows up everywhere, too, but not until he feels he looks reasonably flawless. James St. James' motto "Primp 'till you drop" is the emblematic phrase for all the kids, and so far no one's ever accused Schmidt of falling short in this endeavor. Amazingly, he finds time from all his self-preservation to design and model—and write, too.

An equally early arrival, Richard Alvarez, is a member of Concerned Inc., an organization headed by designer Andre Walker and consisting of kids interested in "fierce visual statements." Individuality is being organized into formal groups like that.

An eighteen-year-old downtown notable named Walter S. has already been the publisher of two fashion magazines, something that could certainly give pause to anyone in his forties who's still searching for a field of achievement. Walter's critiques are not tempered with the caution of age. He shoots from the hip so hard his "attitude" astounds people who don't even have the nerve to say such things in private. And he carries himself with the rude swagger of someone whose every other word is "fierce." As a child (not all that many years ago) in Bayside, Queens, Walter S. didn't read fashion magazines, he devoured them. He later channeled his interest by founding an outlet for his opinionated and highly personal views on both mainstream and up-and-coming designers in the *Key*, a magazine that first appeared when he was a worldly sixteen. The *Key* grew from a meager handout with a circulation of only five hundred to a bigger, slicker extravaganza that cost a dollar a copy and had a circulation of ten thousand. When the publishing company that had picked up the magazine decided to drop it after ten months, Walter S. hardly retired into teenage obscurity. He conceived the *Form*, another iconoclastic fashion magazine, and contributed fashion critiques to other downtown publications at the same time. And, oh yeah, he also designs.

Where there's a will, as they say, there's a way in, and the major domos of the scene are alert enough to know that giving the new talent entree will benefit their own establishments. So, Walter S. got cooperation from clubs that feted his current projects and stores that advertised, and the new infusion of energy helped keep the scene going.

Meanwhile, the older, more established crowd watches with curious fascination and tries to absorb the new energy, or at least make sense out of it, while pragmatically borrowing that skin cream. Andy Warhol, for one, has shrewdly made a career out of continually keeping his finger in the pot of what's bubbling over at the moment. He's worked on projects with Haring and Basquiat and is always on the lookout for the next useful partner. "People misinterpret his stance about life on the planet," says Warhol's friend, makeup artist Way Bandy. "He's always looking forward and looking to have a good time. He's not a downer." Whether he is or not, Warhol's constant interventions have inspired the sixties survivors to feel that they can be more than voyeurs. Hang on long enough and you'll be celebrated yourself, especially now when all sights are fixed on the scene.

Beauregard Houston-Montgomery, who remembers a time when he wanted to "observe the limelight, not be in it," is now being willingly pushed into it, thanks to his androgynous mystique, offbeat personality and obsessively wagging tongue. The breakthrough of pop icons like Boy George helped make outrage a more humdrum everyday emotion, and Beauregard dishes it out gleefully.

This pop sociologist who grew up in Peyton Place—"literally"—went to college for six months during the turbulent sixties. "But I had nothing to protest because we had everything we wanted, so we took drugs." Moving into the heart of the East Village in 1976, he held his twenty-fifth birthday party at astrologer Brien Coleman's loft and was delighted to find it turn into an early high point in downtown party legend. "Patti Smith and the Ramones performed," he enthuses. "Fifteen hundred people showed up, and the doorman, unbeknownst to me, charged them a dollar each and went off to the Islands the next day." He probably would have had more fun staying in the incipient downtown scene.

Beauregard says his life has been largely a reaction against terror. "I was terrified to walk by the Chelsea Hotel, so I moved in. I was terrified to go to Max's, so I went every night." But he's not terrified of the spotlight anymore. In fact, as a guest commentator on "Hot Properties," a cable TV talk show on the Lifetime Network, he approached it with the eagerness of a just discovered starlet. The show broke a

MICHAEL MUSTO 43

• Trilogy of terror or the Three Musketeers? Stephen Sprouse, Andy Warhol and Jean Michel Basquiat (*left to right*) may not look that in touch with each other but, together and separately, they've perpetrated many trends and trademarks.

lot of new ground in presenting downtowners as more chi-chi than freaky. The people shows like "Real People" pointed its fingers at were finally given a chance to prove to a mass audience that they don't belong in a carnival attraction or as displays in the "Carnival" theme at Area. They have brains behind their bravura.

Stephen Saban, one of the founder/editors of *Details* and its nightlife columnist as well as a former club doorman, was actually the first to give the downtown scene credibility. (Some say he created the scene so he could write about it.) In 1985, as *Details*, the monthly New Testament of downtown, grew from a free mailout to a newsstand magazine that reaches over forty thousand readers (grossing in the neighborhood of a million dollars that year), Saban started to reap the rewards of his dedication to 14th Street-and-below. He became recognized as "the Boswell of the night" by *New York Magazine* and "the Noel Coward of the '80s" by *Newsweek*. Publicists started returning his calls, though he didn't always return theirs, and people started recognizing the "nobody's" he insisted on writing about as nobody's worth knowing. He even got a movie gig, consulting on director Joel Schumacher's version of Jay McInerney's novel, *Bright Lights, Big City*, about a guy who compensates for his personal and professional emptiness with long, decadent nights at a New York cafeteria-turned-dance-club called Heartbreak (fictionalized in the book). Saban's hardly ever written about the real Heartbreak—it's not even yesterday's news—but far be it from him, or anyone, to say no to Hollywood, especially when it's a job on what could be one of the hottest movies of the year. Among the elite (and even not so elite) downtown, *Bright Lights, Big City* was the *de rigueur* reading of 1985.

Saban goes out every night of the week, only rarely awarding himself a night off, which means going to only one or two parties instead of the usual three to five. He's one of the few predictable facets of New York nightlife—you know that at every major event, whatever else happens, you'll find him there, skulking around and observing with a crisp understatement. Saban doesn't need to make a spectacle of himself; the spectacle is all around him, and his job is to report it, drawing the line only when he feels the information might interfere with his readers' future fun. Sometimes Saban seems like Marcello Mastroianni in *8 1/2*: besieged by swooning and pleading people cooing his name as he calmly tries to figure his next creative move.

He's often said that when Liz Smith was writing about Steve Rubell, he was chronicling the doings of a darker horse, Steve Mass. Now, of course, they're both writing about Rubell, proving that up and downtown really have converged into a happy union that everyone can be interested in. Liz Smith even writes about Saban sometimes.

The columnist, who was born in England and grew up in Florida, holds a BFA in painting from the Philadelphia

College of Art. He pursued graphic design, however, "because painting was too difficult as a career. Now, of course, it's no problem," he laughs, "but back then you had to be talented and work at it."

After a glittering career designing bootleg T-shirts for rock tours ("You know, the kind they sell seven blocks from Madison Square Garden"), he ran into writer Cynthia Heimel, an old friend who once modeled nude at his college, and she helped him get a job pasting up at the *SoHo News*. In the best Andrew Carnegie tradition, he went on to writing articles for the paper and later landed the editorship of the film section. He became so much a part of the staff that when he was fired by a new editor, the rest of the staff (including the Style editor, Annie Flanders, who later became the publisher of *Details*) went on a twenty-four-hour vigil until the management brought Saban back as a downtown columnist. He did, after all, go to clubs a lot (living above the Baby Doll Topless Go-Go Lounge, he was just a tumble away from the Mudd) and had a droll sense of observation. He rarely takes notes, because, "If I can't remember it, it isn't worth repeating." What's more, anyone who thought of the daily one o'clock installment of "All My Children" as an early morning experience had to be perfect for the life-begins-at-midnight shift.

Stalking the clubs with cool deliberation, Saban looks like the least trendy person out, receiving guests with all the smoothness of the Queen Mother and all the wariness of a producer auditioning Broadway hopefuls. People have been known to go into a Top 40 frenzy for him, singing and dancing their favorite songs at the top of their lamé in shameless attempts to get noticed, only to wilt in humiliation when he excuses himself and walks away in mid-song. One new arrival on the scene admitted his goal in life was to have his picture in Saban's column, and bet a friend he'd make it there first (both made it the same month). In addition to being the casting director of the up-and-coming, Saban's the self-appointed arbiter of morality of the club scene. When he felt a rival columnist was on the Limelight's "emergency" phone too long, he instructed the help to disconnect the phone while the guy was still talking. The help did it.

As the scene's grown in importance, so has Saban, who started out covering much humbler clubs. "The Mudd had no decor, no glamor, no nothing," he says, remembering his first beat. "It was the people who made it happen." And what about those people? Why was he drawn to the Johnny Dynells and Chi Chi Valentis as if only he knew they were the most fabulous creatures in New York? "They're more interesting than the uptown people. They're not afraid of things, and not afraid to say things. They don't hide anything. My goal was to give recognition to them because they got no press at all but were just as valid as any other creative people."

In 1982 along came *Details*, which didn't just give them recognition, it made them into dazzling divas. Suddenly, the selected few found that just as important as the Liz Taylors and Johnny Carsons were the Dianne Brills, Fred Rothbell-Mistas and others who peopled the pages of this "party in a magazine" and make it the breeziest, most hangover-free way to go to a party without going to a party. *Details* is proud to have never run anything about Nicaragua. Unlike *US News & World Report*, the magazine is all glamor, all glitter, all tinsel and precious little news. "I'm absolutely in awe. I really don't understand why people buy it," says Saban, who knows full well.

They buy it because people both inside and outside the scene are more fascinated with it than with the new developments in a TV starlet's love life that they can read about in the weekly tabloids. They buy it because who in the working world has the time or the stamina to schlep out to clubs every night when there's Saban to do it for you? The plight of the young and terminally creative has stirred up so much public interest that no less than three other major publications have been nurtured by a scene most cynics thought was populated by people who couldn't even read. The *East Village Eye*, *New York Talk* and *Paper* provide three totally different approaches to monthly downtown journalism.

The *East Village Eye*—instigated by Leonard Abrams (who once *was* a carnival attraction; he guessed people's weights) with $500 he borrowed from his mother in 1979—"covers independent thought in a cultural context," according to Abrams. "We're by, for and about upstarts—people who have an independent and unique voice in the discourse of human events, whereas *Details* and *New York Talk* are oriented towards fashion and going out. There's a lot of self-expression in fashion, but that's not what those magazines are about. They're about capitalizing on consumer society. I'm interested in what the culture is saying and what we can learn about people through various means of expression."

Abrams can afford his la-de-da attitude. The *Eye* jumped the gun on practically everyone with regard to the East Village buzz. The reason he based the paper in that neighborhood, he says, "was cheap rent, and to give it an image in the public eye. I foresaw the boom."

Walter Thomas, the editor who

● It's been a long night for *Details* man-about-town, columnist Stephen Saban, and the worst thing is that now he has to go home and write about it.

helped establish *New York Talk*, tooted the horn section of *his* publication with equal bombast, saying it covers art "more consistently and better than anything else" (Gracie Mansion has contributed critiques, and some gallery owners have curated art shows within the pages of the magazine), and also features humor pieces, "which a lot of the other papers don't have. At least, not intentionally." So, next to a story about a performer/artist like Keiko Bonk you might find a cute piece about how to torture your dog. A few pages later you'll find Jim Mullen's Hot Sheet column, which can tell you whether Bonk and pet torture are hot, or not, this month. There's no question that the *Talk* is hot, or at least hotter than when it was a mere "shopper" with articles explaining why David Letterman is one of the best-dressed men on TV. Started in 1983, its downtown focus has built a circulation of fifty-five thousand, a statistic that's less impressive when you consider that over 90% of the copies are distributed free in stores and movie theaters. Still, three days after four thousand *Talk*s are placed in Tower Records, the hand-out counter is as bare as a déclassé club on a cash bar night.

Paper might have the most original, if limited, format of all the magazines. It's 9 3/4 by 13 1/2 inches, folds out to 27 by 40 inches, and is filled with short articles on people and things to do, with ads studding the edges of the paper in equal-sized squares. Ex-*SoHo News*' assistant managing editor David Hershkovits is one of four founder/editors—along with Kim Hastreiter, Richard Weigand and Lucy Sisman. "We don't really cover the scene," he says, further differentiating *Paper* from the other publications. "We rarely even print names of scenemakers. But it's downtown in sensibility. It's downtown in the sense that downtown has become a more pervasive element of the whole city. When you say 'downtown,' people think of something. They have an aesthetic idea of what you're talking about. That's what we're about—the downtown aesthetic, not clubbing."

After being jerked around by a publishing company that wanted to put out *Paper*, then reneged, the four enterprising editors decided to do it themselves, chipping in $1000 each for the first issue, which was just the start of this self-motivated forum for their stylistic viewpoints. One of their coups, says Hershkovits, was spotlighting designer Andre Walker before Jean Paul Gaultier and others picked up on him. The clothes they featured "looked like they didn't fit. They were short in the back and long in the front, and vice versa." *Paper* loved them.

Success for such a touch-and-go operation smells like confetti and champagne. If they weren't so busy, the *Paper* perpetrators could pause long enough to laugh in the faces of their could-have-been publishers. But they *are* busy, too busy even to laugh, sneer or just look deadpan at the competing publications' staffers. Anyway, they've finally come to a mutually tolerant situation after some initial backstabbing and rivalry. (If there's any now, it's all done sotto voce.)

"In the beginning, everyone was threatened that we'd have to eliminate each other," says Walter Thomas, who worked at *Details* before *Talk* and says a lot of his writers came from the *Eye*. "But there's been a thaw in our relationships. It's normal now. We're not a threat to each other. In fact, we all make each other legitimate. If there were only one downtown paper, the scene would be considered avant-garde and no one would think it'd last. But since several cover it in different qualitative ways, the scene has more credibility." It's amazing that in addition to preparing new outfits and going out constantly, downtowners have to plow through a veritable library every month. But the potential thrill of finding their own names in boldface, something that might never happen in Liz Smith, makes it sublimely worthwhile.

Search through the names and you'll find the three basic types of downtown boldfaces:

1 **The Hangers-on,** who don't do much of anything except make a spectacle of themselves, thereby continuing the illusion that they're somebodies.

2 **The Flashes-in-the-Pan,** who are created by the media, then knocked down by the same people who grow tired of their not living up to expectations.

3 **The Genuine Achievers,** who are talented and hardworking creative artists for whom going out is just a sidebar, not a way of life.

It's not hard to pick out the names that fall into the first two categories, but the genuine achievers, who are more private and actually have a goal in life beyond getting more drink tickets, are harder to locate. They're usually in the darkest corners of clubs handing out business cards.

John Lurie and Marcus Leatherdale are two good examples of genuine achievers. While Lurie used to go out "to take drugs and pick up girls," he now leaves the house, like practically all the other achievers, because, "If you're out, all these people see you and it seems to generate business." A sax player with the jazz-funk-punk group the Lounge Lizards, he also won notoriety as a star of Jim Jarmusch's acclaimed film *Stranger Than Paradise*, which won the Camera d'Or in Cannes in 1984 and was named best movie of the year by the National Society of Film Critics. That film, he says, in his typical offhand way, was received so well because it was a reaction against Hollywood. "The film's okay, but I don't think it's that great. Sometimes I think, 'My career now is based on that movie's success, the last thing I would have assumed would have gotten me anywhere.'" Lurie found it kind of likable and kind of boring, but critics reacted to it as if they'd never seen an independent film before.

Paradise won him recognition, but not that much money, which might explain why generating business is so

● You can't label John Lurie, who's an actor (*Stranger Than Paradise*), musician (Lounge Lizards) and a shining star in the brigade of out-and-about downtowners who actually do something.

important to Lurie. "For me," he says, "it worked out really badly. I got a percentage of Jarmusch's percentage, which is, like, a long story." Another lengthy yarn is the one about the record company that treated the Lounge Lizards shoddily. "We lost our momentum for a while." Still, he's hardly going to have to live in an Area display. Though he's turned down big-money roles that seemed distasteful to him, he's followed *Paradise* with a Wim Wenders film and another Jarmusch feature. He's also reactivated the Lizards' momentum with an album, "Mutiny on the Bowery," and gigs, which he says are better received outside New York. Because of the social emphasis right now, most clubs don't like to interrupt the steady flow of "Hi, here's my business card" with a live band, unless they're going to sing about a similar theme. "I look back on the first year of the Mudd as the year that changed my life," he says, remembering a time when the arts mingled more spontaneously. "But as F. Scott Fitzgerald once wrote in a story about New York, 'We knew things would never be that much fun again.' Now, clubs are on a bent towards confusion rather than atmosphere."

Details Hidden Identities photographer, Marcus Leatherdale, used to go out nightly to immerse himself in that confusion because he'd be turning it into perfectly logical camera compositions the next day. Now, he can just pile all his photos up and flip them in quick succession and he's got the ultimate downtown party, only prettier and more revealing.

Born and raised in Montreal, Leatherdale studied art there and in California, where he found he was way ahead of the game in every aspect. "The West Coast is more artsy craftsy than the East Coast—there's lots of ceramics and baskets and pottery," says the Monty Clift lookalike. "They told me I was on the wrong coast. I'd put images on the wall about the beginning of the punk era and fights used to break out in class because they thought I was being dishonest. They figured any life other than plants and plant holders couldn't exist."

But for someone like Leatherdale, who had a nimble camera finger if not a green thumb, there was plenty of life outside this macrame twilight zone. In 1979 he made the inevitable move to New York, where he was treated as less of an alien being and did some attention-getting *SoHo Weekly News'* portraits. He got a major break when Jim Fouratt and Rudolf gave him a show at Danceteria. "It was probably the first photo exhibit in a nightclub. A lot of people thought I shouldn't do it because I wouldn't be taken seriously as a photographer. Now, of course, every photographer under the sun is showing in clubs."

Things snowballed from there. He became Stephen Saban's *SoHo News'* photographer, doing character studies of the great unknowns, and showed at Greathouse Gallery, the only photo gallery in the East Village at the time.

He was shown internationally, collected by Vienna's Museum of Modern Art and ascended to the point where his set fees for a commission range up to $700.

"They're all portraits," he says, "but I don't do head shots. I'm working a lot with the body and usually like to show part of the body language. And I don't do nudes unless the focus is less on the nudity than the lines of the body. Sensual, not sexual."

Still, he's anything but a prude. In fact, his work has little to do with the usually pristine world of art photography. He's shed conventions like the idea that every photo should be the same size so an exhibit will look unified. He's joined the vanguard who treat photography more as an art than a science. "Ansel Adams and the other forefathers cared more about the print quality and what a photo should look like," he says, "but the new kids care more about using photography as a creative medium. They're moving to the East Village because that's where they get their chance. Everyone is a lot less academic about their approach."

That approach might never land them on 57th Street, but who says that's where they want to be anyway? "It's not really a goal," says Leatherdale, with typical understatement.

5

«Living It Up and Never Living It Down»

Club d.j. Johnny Dynell waves the flags of freedom—he can spin whatever records he wants in whatever order he feels like it, and he does just that, usually to the crowd's delight.

Going out is more than an exercise in fun for downtown, it's an integral part of life which you must take part in or you're involuntarily retired from the scene like a cancelled check. Clubs are public showrooms where you "get down with your bad self" and take in a full view of everyone else's. At clubs, you embarrass that gallery owner you weren't able to make an appointment with by phone. You can exchange information, phone numbers or something more intimate with all the other notables. You can get photographed, and at least dream of meeting Mr. or Mrs. Right. And if there's time, you can have fun too.

Club hopping exerts such a fascination that it's the focal point of many people's lives. These people would agree that it's not wise to go out every night unless you have to, like Rudolf, who estimates he's had sixty-five thousand nights in a row in clubs (Who's counting?). Of course, most of them feel like they really *do* have to. Staying home is nearly impossible when the stigma of not being seen is even more intense than that of being too visible. Go out and strut around, and people assume you're fabulous. Miss a week of events, and people assume you're dead.

There's tremendous pressure to make appearances and take care of business. There's also the overwhelming fear of missing something. So, most nights at about eight o'clock, the nightlife-compulsives decide that even though they'd spent the whole day assuring themselves that they're staying in, they're going out after all. They have to, they convince themselves, for their own good.

That hardly ends the decision making, though. Their stomachs turn into thousands of tiny Boy Scout knots and their minds work double-time wondering "Where?" Where on earth are they going to go? In New York the choices are both plentiful and absurd—everything from clubs, where you can get physically abused, to Shout! where the tackiness of the crowd might inspire you to be the abuser. Clubs are populated with everyone from B&T's (bridge and tunnels) to LDP's (looks down pat) to GGL's (gotta get laids), from preppies to yuppies to guppies to Tupperware salesladies, from Brooks Brothers types to Village People clones—and the anonymous squad who will adapt themselves into any or all of the above if it'll guarantee their entry into a club. (These people don't even deserve an obnoxious nickname; let's just call them the Anonymous Squad.) They'll all be somewhere tonight, and some of them will be everywhere, which is why a little research is in order before anyone makes that crucial nightlife decision. It's not enough to know what the clubs are like in general, for example. You have to know what they're like on specific nights and even during specific hours of specific nights.

Monday night is deadly. So much so

that some clubs don't even ask for a cover charge (but once you're inside, you'll know why—you get what you pay for). Sunday is a big gay night, which, at the more obvious discos, brings the ever-popular "Tea Dance," where gays dance to Eurodisco starting in the early evening and imbibe everything but tea. At the Pyramid Cocktail Lounge, Sunday brings "Whispers," a weekly theme party which is basically more of the same Pyramid dementia, only a little gayer. Friday and Saturday are the bridge-and-tunnel nights— much dreaded by the trendies—when people come from the boroughs and New Jersey to take over Manhattan, while the weeknights tend to attract a more local and less polyester-pronc crowd. Whatever the night, don't you dare set foot in a club before midnight. You'll instantly be labeled with a scarlet letter "D" for Desperate.

Special events can make even the most hopeless night of the week at the dreariest club into a happening. Unfortunately, these parties and events don't happen every night. So, a thrilling Keith Haring party at Palladium, where some perfectly respectable people couldn't even pay their way in, was followed by a night when the doorpeople were practically Hoover-vac-ing derelicts off 14th Street just to fill the place. Attendance is erratic, to say the least. Of course, part of the Haring party's success was the fact that over four thousand freebies were sent out—the downtown crowd, mostly out of principle, does not like to pay. In fact, practically every major club event nowadays is a comp affair. And usually the patrons are so relieved at having been let in that they instantly run to the bar and celebrate. That makes club owners very happy. The profit from liquor sales is how most of them make their money.

Just as important as the party itself, though, is the party "host" who oversees every aspect of the event like Julia Child would watch a pot of vichyssoise. Alan Rish, for one, knows how to prepare a fancy soup. His mailing list is made up of his twenty-four hundred best "friends" in New York— friends meaning media stars, movers and shakers or potential scene-stealers. "You make cold, calculating decisions," he says. " 'Are these people fabulous?' The really fun ones can fit into every category. They can be outrage or they can be elegant. I even think preppies can stay up all night with the best of them, and are fun in a lot of ways." Well, let's not get too ridiculous, okay?

The Ohio-born, Mexican-raised mailing-list mogul apprenticed under "the Queen of the Comps," cable TV star/party-thrower Nikki Haskell, who it's been joked went bankrupt because she comped too many people. Actually, Haskell went under largely as a result of her cable TV expenses. Rish admires her chutzpah and social talent, if not her bank account. Since working on his own, he's tried to cultivate the delicate balance of aggressiveness, disciplinc and charm essential to a good party host. The revelers only see the crowds and the fun, but being a host involves a lot more—hustling to get the gig, coordinating dozens of variables and working behind the scenes to make sure everyone has a good time. On top of all that, the good host has to make it all seem effortless while concealing a potential nervous breakdown.

Rish's first solo effort was a fete at Underground for the Independent Features Project in 1982. It brought out the likes of Glenn Close and Robert Redford and featured the all-girl percussion band Pulsallama performing "The Devil's in My Husband's Body" as the evening's entertainment. "This was the tail end of the disco era and the Paul Jabaras. Nobody had ever done an uptown promotional event downtown and made it cooler, more esoteric and more interesting than the Hollywood- or Broadway-style party. Downtown had never been exposed to that, the people were used to East Village gallery openings or performance art." The mix was kinda now, kinda wow, and it worked, leading Rish into a full-time career of labeling invitations and licking stamps.

What makes or breaks a downtown crowd, above all, is the crowd those invitations attract. You can have hundreds of waiters serving canapes while a twenty-piece orchestra plays Strauss waltzes, but if the crowd isn't to-die, it's a dud. An interesting mix of people is crucial, and it helps if it's not the same interesting mix as the last few nights. Best of all is an element of surprise—break dancers mingling with high society—and it never hurts to have a few impressive celebrity names, too, because they help create the sense that, "If they're here, this must be an event."

"The celebs are just icing on the cake, though," says Rish sagely. "You can't just say, 'Joan Rivers was there.' There have been awful parties where Joan Rivers was there because she's pushing her book and there are publicists and booksellers and no-fun people. Downtown doesn't go for that. A p.r. party is fun if all you want is a picture in the paper the next morning, but that isn't really a party."

Deciding which celebs will really excite the downtown crowd is no party either, but it's an important part of the intricate planning process. Not that the super cool would exhibit any outward excitement over celebs when they could seem more impressive acting blasé and saying, "Oh, not Greta Garbo again." But don't doubt for a minute that if the name is right, they do feel barely perceptible, but definitely existent, palpitations. Their sneers delicately soften into smirks and their shoulder pads cave in ever so slightly. They're excited.

According to Rish, most soap opera stars, Broadway hoofers and Lorna Luft rate pretty low on the downtown scale. But when a hot new British group arrives, he says, they're definitely "more exciting than Ruth Warrick.... Surviving is not enough. It's doing it with flash and dash, like Tina Turner or Joan Collins. Nothing's more exciting than a flashy breakthrough or comeback. But someone who's just plodding on through the years doesn't thrill me very much.

"The flash and newness is what's appealing. Witness Marilyn. All right, talent doesn't have a lot to do with show business." Oh really? It certainly didn't have much to do with Marilyn's performance at Rish and Way Bandy's party for him at Area, where, discouraged by a sound system that wasn't in control, the British rock star just shrugged his shoulders and walked off, leaving the audience in a profound state of "Wha' happened?" "I loved it," said Marilyn's friend, Bandy. "At least he got some prima donna p.r. out of it." Not many agreed that the stunt was so lovable, but no one could say it didn't draw a great mix of people out for "the flash and newness." And Marilyn's friend, Boy George, was obviously impressed. When one reveler opined that Marilyn's going to be a big star, George suddenly clammed up as if a raw nerve had been hit. Do British pop-star/best-friends duos really get jealous?

While contemplating that, you could have talked to a startling diversity of stars, from Sandra Bernhard to Andrew Stevens to . . .yes, Joan Rivers (minus her publicists), or reveled in the emphatic posturing for the downtown paparazzi of the dowager empress of New York nightlife, Dianne Brill, who, in addition to being a substantial figure in fashion, is also renowned for having bosoms at least as impressive as John Sex's hair. Brill, she of the twin towers and the towering personality, gives her benediction—a juicy "Mwah!"—to swarms of people who line up for it, as if her approval alone will make them more valid on the scene. And, strangely enough, it does.

The Tampa, Florida-born diva is a natural hostess, combining the surfer spirit with a poignantly dizzy *La Dolce Vita*-inspired impression of following the crowd, fully aware that she's actually leading it. An airhead she's not. Backed by Gary Bogard—*Details'* financial angel—Brill's line of men's clothing now gets wide retail distribution. And in her corsetlike Jayne Mansfield dresses that are so tight they look like they're painted on, she's nothing if not photogenic. Brill has such a visual impact on people, her former assistant Ica (pronounced Izza) Mueller molded herself into an eerily identical physical image. The downtown press have frequently run photos of them both in full bodacious splendor.

As long as the cameras keep snapping, the party's a success. And if the party's a success, Rish is usually left with a feeling of total dread at the end of the night. How is he going to top it? "You don't do something for a month," he says, "and people say, 'Is Alan Rish dead?' It's very up and down. At times you're really hot and Andy Warhol says, 'You give the best parties, and I love you' and at other times you go through lulls." Even in the good times, he says, "I can get a good table at a restaurant, but many times I can't pay the bill. It's a little ironic, no?" It's a little ironic, yes.

Like practically everyone else on the

scene, Rish wants to parlay his social skills into big business. "A party is really like putting together a deal, organizing all these complicated things and dealing with everyone from busboys to presidents. I want that to lead to something substantive someday. I hope it leads to major deal making."

If he looked around he'd see major deal making happening at every single minor downtown party. Stand still for five minutes and you're accosted by people furtively handing out flyers for their own events at other clubs. No one's content to just enjoy the current event as a self-contained evening of fun. It's seen as a promotional ground for the future. So, people carry bags in which they collect the invitations which the most innocent remark can provoke these tireless self-promoters to pull out. (A: "I'm so depressed." B: "Here are some invitations to my fashion show. Maybe they'll cheer you up.")

If you were to flee the self-promotional barrage and take refuge in, let's say, the ladies' room, you'd hardly find a quiet and relaxing retreat. You'd find the heart of the action. Somehow, the ladies' room has evolved into the best room in practically every club, where people go to escape the loud music and just let it hang. Hardly anyone is a lady in here, even if they're female, and no one really cares. The point is to let loose with more abandon than would be advisable in the more out-in-the-open areas of the club. Then, wash yourself off in the sink.

Look into the stalls and you'll see dozens of happy feet attached to the gremlins who are trick-or-treating for nose candy or doing Ecstasy and hoping it will live up to its name and not drop them wickedly in the night. The drug exchange is intense, but these people can't seriously be doing anything productive with their lives if this is a nightly ritual for them. As columnist Jim Mullen wise-assed about Ecstasy in *New York Talk*, "I brain damage hear it cause can."

If the ladies' room is too deep a slice of life for you, you could always venture back to semi-civilization—usually the back room—where there's plenty of mind-boggling delirium to experience even without the benefit of drugs. Here you can get high on life, or crash on

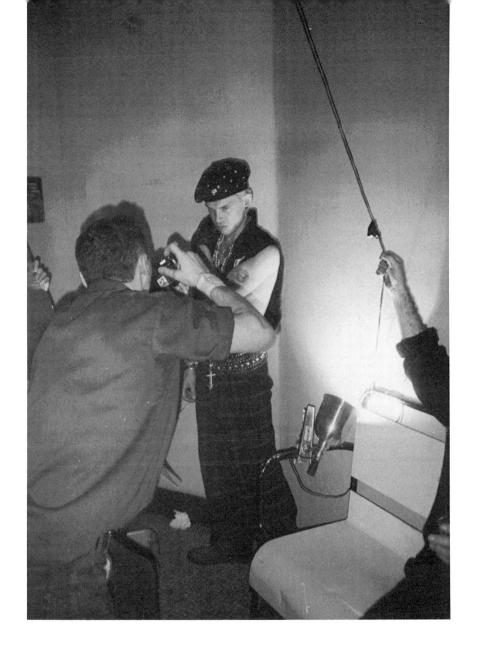

● A lot of things happen in Area's john, toiletry not normally among them. Here, photographer Stephan Lupino shoots sneering rocker Billy Idol for a series of people-of-the-night-in-the-loo.

sheer absurdity. "I thought of a great opening line for a short story," mysterious socialite (What does he do, anyway?) Julian de Rothschild-Blau says during the twenty-minute wait for a drink. " 'I married my rapist!' " Then he trails off with double-fisted vodka and cranberries, leaving the story's development, climax and denouement to your own imagination. But you left your word processor at home, and this party is more vivid than any short story anyway. Here you could find connubial bliss with your own rapist (that could be your next event) or at least enjoy the search. "Ohmigod!" A prominent East Village gallery owner is fingering the behind of an otherwise fashionable eighteen-year-old boy, stopping only when he realizes a potentially vicious gossip columnist has been watching them in action all along. A ridiculously obese club doorman is walking around in clothes he procured from his mother's closet the minute she fell asleep.

David Ilku is telling the person who called him "David Lovechild" that that's only one character in his repertoire, he's only a part-time psychedelic. Sydney T. Masters, a buxom girl with a curious British accent (curious because she's not from England), is looking for her life supports, Boy George and Marilyn. Later, she yells at people to leave them alone, even though it seems they *are* alone. A club owner is explaining why he only sleeps with dominatrixes, and a girl is screaming at the top of her lungs just to prove that she can. Sally Randall, an aspiring superstar celebrated for her outrageous wigs and hats, is saying, "Can't we exchange this crowd for another one?" On stage, someone is doing a serious tribute to James Bond theme songs. The evening's deliriously fun, but everyone's too busy thinking they might be missing something better somewhere else to enjoy it.

Who let all these fabulous looney tunes in? Probably Haoui Montaug, who's worked the door at so many clubs, people ask for him even at places he's never heard of. (The cry of "Haoui! Haoui!" sounds up all along New York nights like a sick coyote's howl.) Montaug is the casting director who orchestrates the crowds as if choosing actors for a Lina Wertmuller film. He's worked everywhere from Bond's ("They caught on for two weeks when the Clash played there") to Interferon ("They paid my plane fare to Europe, so they were fine") to the reopened Studio 54 ("Only for two months, which was long enough") to Palladium ("I don't let in girls exposing themselves to get guys, or guys looking for girls exposing themselves"). He says that except for having to stand out in the cold, "Working the door is almost amusing. The people who annoy me are almost the ones I enjoy the most."

Montaug's so amused by these late-night annoyances, he's gone to the trouble of breaking them down into five basic types:

1 The Pushers: They claw their way to the front where they effect a look that says, "Don't you know who I am?" They are usually asked to push their way back to New Jersey.

2 The Whiners: They say things like "But I wore my best shoes!" in a voice so irritating you have to let them in just to shut them up.

3 Everybody's Friends: They are the people who say they're the brother of the makeup artist of the band's road manager and then wait for applause for this staggering accomplishment.

4 The Waiters: Their entrance technique is to just stand there for hours with a glum face and try to work on the doorman's potential for guilt.

5 The Entitled: They feel that since they bused the tables at El International (a trendy TriBeCa tapas restaurant), they are now entitled to go to every club for free for the rest of their lives.

All five groups along with the genuinely entitled party people—the Fabulous 500—make the scene. Sometimes.

Partly as a refuge from all these mad types, Montaug's been producing Danceteria's *"No Entiendes"* cabaret, which stars many of these same people in a sort of downtown "Gong Show" (minus the gong, alas), for four years. His goal is to have a transatlantic comedic flying circus of the 1990s, but right now it's just a series of performers perpetrating often humiliating acts on a voracious crowd. Whether they humiliate themselves or the crowd depends on how quick they are on the offensive. The shows are an outrage—not necessarily the best downtown performers, but definitely the ones that'll provoke a cheer (Bronx or otherwise) in three minutes or less. Madonna gave her first club performance at this perennial event and the rest is history of the sort that defines the meaning of *'No Entiendes''*—you don't understand.

Karen Finley, a performance artist, sometimes intones an absurdly funny, pornographic tone poem that goes, "And we sniffed all the Rolaids . . . and I wanted her . . . and I shoved my fist up her . . . and she had her period." That's a crowd pleaser. But two guys doing "The Beer Hunter" (a takeoff on *The Deer Hunter*), in which they play Russian roulette with beer cans, is a bit esoteric for this crowd. Your hosts, by the way, are Montaug and Anita Sarko, who are shamelessly dressed as murder victim Eigil Vesti and suicide victim the Singing Nun. Montaug likes to keep the show topical and lively. "We want to arouse more than offend," he says, "but if people get offended along the way, that's okay. Stephen Saban said he found the Vesti show one of the ultimately tasteless statements, and he wasn't even there." Montaug glows.

At Area, where theme installations change every five weeks, they aren't quite so pleased with their own irreverence. Though the owners originally told their ex-resident performer Zette (offstage name, Albert Joseph Bernard

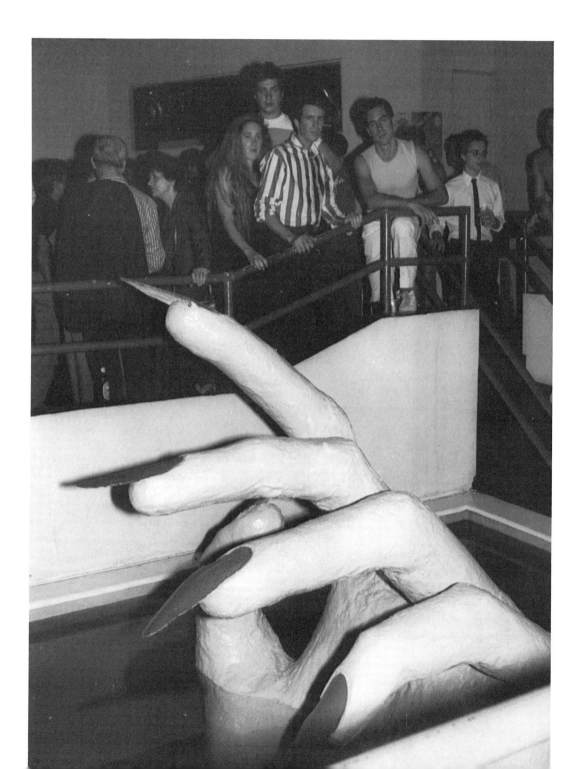

> • The giant Fiberglas hand (by artist Michael Stats) gives the fingers to all the trendies and attitudinizers at Area, and only the ultraobservant will notice that the long,

> colorful nails fit in with that month's "Red" theme. Co-owners Chris and Eric Goode and Darius Azari (*left to right*) will turn red if the club becomes a past trend.

III) to go as far as he wanted with his theme-related characterizations, they got nervous when he planned to be crucified for the "Confinement" theme around Easter time.

All dressed up with nowhere to be nailed, Zette had to settle instead for sitting in the same outfit in a crib made for hyperactive retarded children. "It bugged me because I wanted to show people who were confined yet strong in character, not cowering or whimpering," whimpered Zette. He followed it up in later weeks with his versions of Rapunzel, Quasimodo, Anne Frank and an anonymous woman under a hair drier. When the "Faith" theme came along (not around Easter time), Zette finally got to live his crucifixion dream—he was St. Sebastian tied to a tree, and still has the scars all over his chest from the bloody arrows he glued onto himself to prove it. That's called suffering for one's performance art.

Zette's immaculately thought-out personality schisms along with the club's $30,000-plus switches in decor helped make Area a club with constant visual stimulation, even when people are just offering flyers and not drugs. For the "Sci-Fi" theme, he was a flawless Jane Jetson at her control board surrounded by set designs that looked like they were straight out of *Plan Nine from Outer Space*. The "Carnival" theme turned him into half a set of Siamese twins (the other half was a mannequin joined to him by the braid) in a sprawling, wonderfully sleazy environment of Pierrots, midgets and temporary tatoos. Other times he could be anything from Joan of Arc to Joan Carrington Colby of "Dynasty."

"We didn't want something everybody will be bored with, or we'd get bored with," says Shawn Hausman, one of the club's four owners (along with Darius Azari and brothers Christopher and Eric Goode), explaining how the club's found stability in constant change. "People have short attention spans, and the element of surprise is always good." As he says that, a three-dimensional Vietnam-related painting emits a deafening bang. It's part of the "Art" theme.

Zette's attention span has to be at least four-and-a-half hours because that's how long he's frozen into charac-

ter. "I just tell myself I'm not going to move" he says, "and do so only once in a while, hopefully when no one's looking. The worst is when you're sitting there and this cute guy is standing next to you and you can't talk. Even if he's still there at four-thirty, he won't recognize me out of costume. In the first year I worked at Area, I went home with someone only one time." That's one more than most people at Area.

But probably more distressing are the people who stare him down, waiting for him to blink, or who are disappointed "if I don't do a tap dance or something welcoming them to the club." Still, the performer, who's done everything from designing shoestore windows to working with Christine Valmy skin-care products to selling Halloween costumes, says sitting still at Area was better than sitting still most other places. "I love people-watching, and I have the most fantastic vantage point for that."

He can see Prince's army of bodyguards harass photographers who dare to snap the Purple One's likeness. Strangely enough, the rock star came to this crowded downtown event to be left alone and has just come from Limelight, where he reportedly was surrounded by those same guards as he danced with his favorite partner, himself. Zette can see Cyndi Lauper feverishly imagining how she could redo the club with her own ideas. And her publicist, Susan Blond, says, "I bring all the groups here, to introduce them to all the right people and show them how sexy New York is. It's an added thrill when they see the crowd part like the Red Sea when I approach." Blond is almost as famous as some of her acts. And whether they're famous or not, everyone here acts it, posing and oozing attitude you could cut with a drink ticket.

Area, done without big-time backing, brought in over $3 million a year in its prime by fusing disparate elements of New York nightlife into an inspired multimedia mélange. The fearless foursome of owners tried out some of their sicker ideas in a fourth-floor walkup they held demented parties at in 1981. (One night, they decorated the place with an eel tank, forty fresh bones dangling from the ceiling, and two live rabbits in a display case.) Now they're perpetrating more refined themes onto the Area crowd. Everything is elaborately planned, down to the invita-

● Area performer Zette (offstage name Albert Joseph Bernard III) loses his head as Marie Antoinette at Area's October '84 "Fashion" theme.

tions—which could be a pill that dissolves in water, leaving just the required information, or a box of Cracker Jack with a surprise inside. The combustion of the crowd and Johnny Dynell's d.j.-ing are what make it a totally spontaneous evening. Dynell has been known to mix a Martin Luther King speech behind a funk beat, play hours on end of opera or spin his own street-funky records. His music doesn't please everyone, though. Least of all *New York Magazine*, who called it "shockingly retro bass-heavy disco—the sort of sound you find in second-rate nightspots around the world." Of course, this is the same publication that called Kenny Scharf "the bearer of the bad news" in a piece about cultural faddism and cheap thrills in art. And if you do find the same sound in second-rate discos, it's probably because they're imitating Area.

Mark Kamins, a d.j. who's produced records for Dynell and Madonna and spun at various clubs, says, "Dance music went through a transition in 1980 when a lot of English bands first heard James Brown and a lot of funksters first heard Joy Division." These relevations led to an open-door policy, whereby makers of dance music were mutually influenced and inspired, and rock, funk, rap and disco both fused and coexisted peacefully. While Malcolm McLaren made people dance to square dance music and opera, nightclubbers found they could also move their feet to salsa, African music and even contemporized versions of the music their parents danced to. "I just play music for people who want to dance and scream," says Kamins. He's willing to spin whatever will provoke that reaction.

Too bad a lot of club d.j.'s resort to the easiest reaction-getter—Top 40. And too bad most of the downtown crowd would rather mix and mingle in the exclusivity of a VIP room (the ultimate exercise in snob appeal, where you have to be on a list within a list to merit admission) than dance. Here the music filters in more softly. It is a soundtrack for people-watching, not for choreographic orgasms. Your arousal is based purely on self-importance—yours and that of the other VIPs, who are almost as flashy and famous as you are, but let's face it, not quite. Some of them even have jobs and all of them have at least 365 potential outfits a year.

On a good night at Limelight—

> • When Zette takes off his costume (and shirt), he's a mesmerizing persona of his own, singing songs like "The Beauty of Pain" at spots like the Cat Club.

● Fred Rothbell-Mista, Limelight's VIP traffic controller and all-around lovable wiseass, sometimes wears this sweater listing all the questions people invariably ask him, so, in case they forget their lines, Fred can act as a life-sized cue card. The club's Claire O'Connor knows all the answers.

housed in a 137-year-old structure that served as a drug rehabilitation center before it converted to discoism—the VIP Room can be the best club in town. It's a place where confessions are in order, but none are offered unless it'll get you a drink. Set in a dimly lit library in the upper reaches of the club, the room seats rock stars, models and downtown royalty on banquettes that can be roped off so that ordinary VIPs don't intrude on the VI-VIP's. These people are made to feel that the church was built in worship of them.

You won't see owner Peter Gatien running around this room very often. He travels a lot to his other clubs, and even when he's around, he's hardly the mix-and-mingle type. Does he dislike people? "No," says Fred Rothbell-Mista, who takes care of the VIP's here, "He's just not a phony. He won't kiss ass. If he doesn't like a press person, he won't be nice to them. He's one club owner who's honest. Everybody gets paid on the books. He's not looking to get laid, get high or meet celebrities. It's a breath of fucking fresh air."

Rothbell-Mista lords over this room like a hyperprotective den mother—keeping mental files of who deserves what and why, and cursing out his underlings when they don't grovel at the right people. Drool buckets should be placed around the room to catch the nocturnal emissions of the help in their most delightfully obsequious moments. But they're the only fidgety ones here. The room is vibrant but relaxed, never reflecting Rothbell-Mista's Machiavellian plottings of who should be let in, who should get champagne instead of just cocktails and who should be escorted up and down the stairs as protection from the essence-de-Rahway, New Jersey, that sometimes emanates from the dance floor. Nouvelle chanteuse Phoebe Legere tinkles something reassuring on the piano and somehow all is well.

Rothbell-Mista is frantically efficient and brutally direct. When someone grabs him from behind and says, "Fred, I need . . .", he retorts, "You got it!" and gives them the finger. "If someone's nice to me, I don't care if they're a superstar or a janitor," he says, "I'll be nice to them. But I find it rude when people treat me like a personal valet. I'm not a focal point for people's glamor. It's never the Ron Woods, by the way, who are annoying. It's their friends, groupies, roadies and families."

He started as a downstairs doorman, where his policy was also to encourage the less aggressive types. "I'd spot a Rolex watch or a guy in blue jeans in the back and pull him through. The guy in the rented limo and the rented tux who says, 'Excuse me. Is Vanessa here?' would have to wait for ten or fifteen minutes." The self-professed Don Rickles of downtown ("It shocks people that I'm so honest. But I can look anybody in the eye in New York.") conceived the VIP Room so that "a hundred people can be snotnosed and the rest can get down and dance."

With the church's parish meeting halls and nun's quarters redone into dancing, dining and mingling areas, Limelight caused a scandal when it opened in 1983. "We are horrified" exclaimed the Right Reverend Paul Moore, Jr., the Episcopal Bishop of New York. Of course, that comment only helped grease the wheels of the club's publicity machine. Though the club never made a big thrilling splash—it became swingles heaven much too soon—it's been swathed in publicity and hosted some unique events: everything from a "Disco Hospital" theme party (where the guests needed mental help by the end of the evening), to Tish Gervais' "TV Star Search" (a transvestite beauty pageant) to an "Egg" night, with Perri Lister sensually cracking hundreds of eggs on a willing muscleman sitting in a bathtub on stage. "Why?" the dazed patrons wondered, to which the only appropriate answer was "Why not?"

The club—the only one open seven nights a week—has something else over Area. Limelight changes their theme practically every night, not every five weeks. Their changes, however, are not as elaborate, and you always know it's Limelight.

Whatever it is, they must be doing something right. Gatien, who already had a Limelight in Fort Lauderdale and Atlanta (both of which he sold), has spread his empire to London and Chicago as well. Could Limelight become the McDonald's of nightlife, with God knows how many billion served? No. Gatien insists the empire won't strike back after these three times. Besides, invoking the Lord's name in this case would probably provoke the Right Reverend again.

Actually, Palladium might be even closer to that goal with just one outlet—the place is humungous, holding as many as thirty-five hundred people in its 104,000 square feet. The figure-conscious will also be excited to know that the 14th Street former opera house, built in 1926, contains seven floors, three bars and fifty video screens—all in a state-of-the-art extravagance most clubs only dabbled in before. Those video screens, for example, don't all just show the same thing (though they can); they each show one component of a total picture, so that all together they add up to one amazingly large image that hovers over the dance floor like a Big Brother-style conscience urging you to keep dancing. It's almost as divinely creepy as dancing at Limelight, with the altars and stained glass windows in full view.

But comparisons are hardly relevant. Palladium's so expensive looking and so goddamned big that every other hot club instantly faded to room temperature the second it opened. And despite fears that it would be a retro dance palace that would make the trendies feel like they'd been thrown back ten years by a time tunnel, the club managed to house dozens of ultraknowing, downtown events in its first season. As a result, they cut a bit into the cutting edge of the other clubs. Area, for all of its ingenuity, became a sort of anticlimax after Palladium, and when its owners stripped the club bare before closing for the month of August in 1985 and decided to make that bareness a mock theme called "The Emperor's New Clothes," a lot of the regulars were ready to stop being regulars.

After making Loretta Young entrances into all of Palladium's Disneyland-like clubs-within-a-club and twirling madly until they almost became part of the art installations, the Fabulous 500 looked at Area's blank walls and went, "Huh?" But Area, at least, reeks of downtown authenticity. It caters profusely to downtown. Palladium's more like an absentee parent who would like you home for the holidays, but could live without you. And the glitter palace was bound to acquire the same eventual tarnishing, but that's the way it is in a scene where when one place is hot it means at least five or six others aren't. Also, once the summer of '85 was over, the club went after the uptown, back-from-the-Hamptons crowd more decidedly. This made downtown feel a bit like they'd been had.

"Physically, the club is brilliant," says James St. James. "But lately they tend to cater more to the uptown crowd. When you ignore the downtown kids, you don't have much of a club because we're the ones the people from New Jersey come to look at." James, it should be added, is there at least twice a week.

Palladium is "conceptually consulted" (i.e. run) by Studio 54 masterminds Steve Rubell and Ian Schrager, proving that even though a club manager's life span is usually under five years, he can almost always resurrect him or herself with a new project. Rubell, a feisty little man whose hair fell out from nerves just before the Palladium's big opening (later it grew back), wanted the ultimate mix of uptown, downtown and in-between. That's the reason why the club places its hotsy-totsy trappings alongside aesthetic environments that appeal to the art-conscious, juxtaposing dozens of blinking lights with the trendiest of art works.

"Wine, women, song—boys, girls, whatever you're into" is Rubell's motto. "People have problems all day. They don't want to have them all night too." Rubell goes so far as to instruct security guards to just stand there and smile if rowdies start beating up on them. "It's a place for fun," he enthuses. To each his own.

"What makes the club work," adds Rubell, "is that there are different environments for different people, as opposed to the late seventies when everybody liked one thing. That was the 'me' decade. Now it's the 'we' decade—people want to mix with a lot of different types. A club has to be more than a big room with a lot of lights. It has to capture the moment, and there are various moments happening right now. The art is a tremendous contributing factor in what makes the club work." He feels artists are to this decade what designers were to the last one and rock stars were to the one before that. So, among other things, the club is a veritable shrine to new and trendy art. In the upstairs Mike Todd Room (so named because it was once the famous producer's office), there are frescoes painted by Jean Michel Basquiat that add to the room's perfectly preserved sense of elegant decay, inspired by Jean Cocteau's movie *Beauty and the Beast*. On the bottom level, there's an outrageous Kenny Scharf fantasy rec room teeming with colorful artifacts of contemporary culture that assault the senses with tchotchkas, brightness and absurdity. The room has been called both '60s and '90s; it's frantic psychedelia, as retro as it is futuristic. The public phones in there are totally usable, if you can stop laughing at the toy monsters and other objects attached to the receivers long enough to pick up and dial. Elsewhere in the club, there are contributions by the likes of Keith Haring and Francesco Clemente, all underlining the fact that a club has to be more than a club to entice the "I've seen it all and my dear I'm still here" downtown crowd. There's even a musty old generator area they thought about opening, as an antidote to all the calculated fabulousness elsewhere. Of course it's just as calculated as everything else. Palladium hasn't missed a trick in its crowd attracting tactics because above all, the place is a business—a business that depends on large numbers of people having expensive fun on a regular basis. As Rubell admits, you can have all the glittering technology money can muster, but if you don't have the stimuli to draw the right crowd, the club's not only a crashing bore, it's a financial fizzle. And 3,500 of the wrong people can be extremely boring. So, after booking events he thinks won't induce yawns, Rubell and his staff draw from the quarter-million names separated into 38 subdivisions of the mailing list (fashion, art, uptown, downtown, gay, etc.), and decide which people from which lists will make a certain party not just crowded, but actually a happening. "It's become a mail order business," says Rubell. "Last month alone, we sent out 240,000 invitations." Thank God all the recipients didn't show up.

Those variables change every single night. For a private Liza Minnelli party, the place teems with celebs—Halston, Ty Power, Jr., Rebecca De Mornay, Sandy Duncan, plus dozens of others—but for a Stephen King pre-Halloween party shortly after that, the club's suddenly less glamorous than spine-tinglingly spooky, from the decor on down to the eerie-looking clientele right out of *Pet Semetary*. The club can have three events at once—a Debbie Harry party "Backstage" (the area behind the dance floor, which the architects purposely made even starker and dingier than it was when they found it), a socialite-oriented fashion show on the main dance floor area, and a party for famed illustrator Antonio in the Mike Todd Room, which d.j. and "atmospheric engineer" Anita Sarko likens to a chi-chi version of the local bar—a cool place to hang out and *let* it hang out. Her music is every bit as eccentric as the room. She won't play "Incense and Peppermints" by the original group, Strawberry Alarm Clock, but she'll play the version by a group called the Adult Net ("Actually," she explains, "they were a slightly different version of a group called The Fall"). "This," she adds, "would never appeal to a Wham! audience." It doesn't matter; they're all downstairs anyway.

Up here, twenty-nine mirrors, hanging curtains and bistro-like tables make the room what many downtowners say is "the nice place you want to meet friends at and can never find." Of course, on some nights, "nice" is a bellydancer gyrating with a candelabra on her head (for that Antonio party) or a rock star ripping off a guy's T-shirt and writing his phone number on the guy's chest and screaming, "Call me!"

The room acts as a private club-within-a-club where, strangely enough, no doorman is needed to keep it exclusive. The cool crowd—the core of any club—levitate here like iron filings to a magnet. Though the prevailing wisdom is that no one dances anymore, you *can* dance if you want to up here. You can also relax, sit, mingle, pose, look in the mirrors and wonder if it's still Stephen King night. Downstairs, everyone seems to look the same. In the Mike Todd, the thrill of seeing and being seen multiplies with practically every person that enters. Here, fun is photographed and hyped, ogled and appreciated. "Look at me when I'm talking to you," a girl in a Dynell wig says to her date, but he's too busy surveying the room. Can you blame him? Dean Johnson's in a minidress living the title of his new song, "Attitude." Tish Gervais is dancing on a tabletop and getting lots of exposure. An older man is offering to take pictures of people with his pet Macaw. Two Yuppies look confused. Racing from one part of the club to another, you not only feel like you're in the ultimate shopping mall of New York nightlife, you also feel like you've accomplished a week's worth of exercise. Whether your mind is exercised in any way is up to what you do between running.

If Palladium succeeds in capturing the current moment (or moments), it's because it seems to have all the accoutrements and gimmicks of previous clubs and comes up with a few new ones too. It fulfills the most important criteria for the jaded: Every few steps it reminds you of why you're not going to leave to go somewhere else, despite recurring symptoms of that nightlife-compulsion. Unfortunately, Palladium's success has led to a frenetic, circus-like atmosphere that's based less on having fun than on having fun in dozens of ways and with thousands of

people. And Rubell has actually said the place is a response to people's need to be "intimate"!

That's the reason why, when downtowners come up with their own alternatives to the big, expensive clubs, they create funky, unpolished places where you can't even see yourself in the mirrors, let alone the walls. These clubs are places where the core crowd can interact without zillions of gadgets, glitter balls and uptown snobs blurring their vision. In the East Village, bars and performance spaces pop up with names like King Tut's Wa Wa Hut, Darinka, Save the Robots, the Aztec Lounge (a Pyramid offshoot) and Downtown Beirut (which is so dilapidated it's probably just what downtown Beirut is really like) whose entire charm derives from the fact that they don't pretend to be very alluring. There are no VIP rooms or drink tickets, but there is still snob appeal. It's based on anti-chic—the more authentic the grunge encrusted under your fingernails is, the more fabulous you are.

So, climbing a smoky stairway to get to a crowded, un-air-conditioned 14th Street American-Legion-headquarters-turned-Thursday-night-cocktail-lounge became one of 1985s most statusy downtown things to do. The popularity of co-host Edwige (a sometime Gaultier model and transplanted Parisian luminary) and the need for a different kind of club made the cozier and more cabaretlike Beat Cafe happen alongside the mammoth and more impersonal dance palaces uptown.

"Tony Catania, my partner, and I wanted to do a club that was exactly like a B-movie hangout," says Edwige, "with a lot of smoke and a torch singer in the background. We started looking around, and came up with this." "This" was a narrow, rickety space with Madonna posters on the wall next to minishrines to Elvis; a sign on the bar that said, "I'm not a dirty old man, I'm a sexy senior citizen"; and American Legion bartenders who, dirty or not, looked both shocked by the drastic transformation of their place and delighted by it. As the weeks went by, one of the older bartenders started jazzing up his outfits in an adorable attempt to keep up with the dressed-to-kill patronage. "One week," laughs Edwige, "he wore a silver lamé tie to be, like, disco."

The torch singer in the club is Edwige herself, who, in addition to modeling, nightclubbing and writing po-

> • For the bridge-and-tunnel people whose true allegiance is to Brooklyn clubs like 2001, Palladium has a special drop that descends, recreating that very place.

etry, is devoted to pursuing a career as a vocalist. It's not surprising that the girl who prefers Chanel suits to trendy new styles also likes classic music—her repertoire contains Marlene Dietrich songs and other smoky barroom favorites. She sang these songs in the club backed by a combo who set up on an impromptu stage in the far corner of the room. If you couldn't always hear her so well, it was because the cozy cabaret had become so popular it nearly exploded with people and the more ridiculous of them could be heard screaming at the doormen over the $2 admission. Asking these people to pay $2 for an evening's entertainment is as insulting as asking them to pay $20. Royalty doesn't pay, even if they're just royal pains in the ass. "But it's only two bucks," said Edwige, harried by her own triumph, "and it's to pay the band. People are calling me to get on the list, and I don't even have a list." Edwige made a lot of friends with the Beat Cafe, and risked losing some too.

The club, which was eventually extended to two nights a week, moved to other locations (including a fabulously seedy place of dubious repute called Carmelita's Reception House) and became a dependable bastion of transience, much like Area. Edwige's only regret, she said at the time, was that *she* was doing the Beat Cafe "because it's the kind of club I'd like to go to."

She probably also liked 8 B.C., a crowded, atmospheric place that was "not really a performance space and not really a nightclub," according to Cornelius Conboy, a co-owner. Whatever it was, the place was a local delight, a welcome respite from glitter balls and Dom Perignon. They avoided the three-piece suit/linen dress crowd by not advertising and defied the trendies, who only want to go to a club because it's "hot," by making the place continually sizzle with a steady stream of intriguing, if sometimes crackpot, performers. But regrettably, once the club got national recognition in magazines like *Vogue*, the trendies did come and so did the city who declared it "unlicensed" and slammed its doors down. They presented no less than 1,500 performances in their first two years in this glorified warehouse, which was livened up by murals and some cheerfully unpretentious people who appreciated the old college try, but refused to take it when a British group called the Lulu Revue did a musical history of the twentieth century. Putting lampshades on their heads while dancing the Charleston for the twenties segment, the Lulus prodded the crowd with burst of "Come alive, you morons!"—but fabulous people do not enjoy the suggestion that they're morons. Oh well—1,499 intriguing performances in two years isn't bad.

Conboy and Dennis Gattra bought the building in 1979 in hopes of turning it into an off-off-Broadway theater, "but what we were thinking of in terms of theater then had to be presented in a club context in 1984." Their backgrounds are bizarrely ideal, if you can believe them. According to Gattra, he ran away to join a traveling circus when he was sixteen, and "Cornelius managed and designed whorehouses. So, we're a serendipitous partnership combining a complete range of the entertainment industry."

And their booking policy had just the wacky eclecticism you'd expect from such a duo: a play called *Whatever Happened to Bernhardt Goetz?* (the title character marries Marilyn Monroe, with whom he "honeymoons through history") was followed a few days later by an "all-Hassidic tribute to Ozzy Osbourne." A "blues/raunch pop band" that promised a big sailor turnout came not long after with *The Unsilent Scream*, "a talking cunt production."

The place was clearly a less frenetic but no less avant-garde Pyramid, a little closer to the edge of Manhattan, and everything else. And a former catering hall off Avenue C proved just as close to the edge when Arthur Weinstein and others opened it as The World to an unassuming crowd who found it a large and comfortable museum of unwitting paradoxes—the stark and the kitschy, a car crash display across a huge, glittering chandelier—that provided a nice local alternative to the calculated dazzle elsewhere.

Other nightclub possibilities are virtually endless. A mere 104,000-square-foot nightclub with art, descending sets and fifty video screens is fabulous, ho-hum, but to generate that extra spark of fascination, it helps to set a club somewhere truly different—like a bowling alley, pool hall, moored boat or pizza parlor—all of which have been done. So have parties on the Coney Island boardwalk, which Bobby Bradley and the Pyramid drag brigade took over while Vito Bruno continued to host his short but scintillating "outlaw" fetes in lovely locales like the 57th Street garbage pier. That event was an olfactory nightmare, but a celebratory delight for at least three other senses. Some claimed Vito had his fete accompli for Annie Flanders on the Williamsburg Bridge just so the reveling hordes could block the uncalled-for bridge-and-tunnel people from coming over. Actually, it was held there just because it hadn't been done before (and judging from the police response, will probably never be done again). The propensity for outrageousness in nightlife is so strong that all of Liberace's "dancing waters" spouting and effusing in a large department-store-turned-nightclub called Bond's failed to make downtown even bat a collective eyelash. The club just didn't have it.

No matter what kind of club we're talking about, the evening doesn't take care of itself after the crucial but hardly all-encompassing moment of entry. If anything, the possibilities just begin to open up like so many dormant flowers coming to life under the heat of track lighting. Almost immediately, the "Where?" is logically followed by "Who?" and "What?"—and most important of all, "Why?" If you can't answer these questions with reasonable alacrity, then you should have stayed home with the A Team instead of trying to compete with the "A" list, though you'll quickly find there's plenty of room on the "would-B" list if you slip up.

Club behavior is a complex and elaborate science, with its own rules and wisdoms that are either acquired through years of experience with swizzle sticks and coatcheck rooms or just through common sense and a little imparted wisdom. The more you know, the better armed you'll be against potential career and social suicide, acts you won't want to commit without the appropriate camera crew in attendance. Which brings us to the first "Why?" of going out. Publicity. There are people who go out just to get mentioned and photographed—and they're usually the same people who later complain that they're not taken seriously in their particular field. But it's just not right for a neurosurgeon to be guzzling Mai Tai's and spinning those little parasols as he does the funky chicken every night in hopes of getting mentioned on page 6 of the *New York Post*. Stick to the medical journals.

Other reasons for leaving the house may be among the following:

1 *To get picked up.* This timeless phenomenon helps keep clubs going as glorified dating services. But anyone who uses dance floors as mating grounds is in for well-deserved trouble. The sea of potential dates is depressing enough to make you celibate for life. If they're readily available, chances are they've either embraced more partners in an evening than you'll know in an entire lifetime or they're bowwow babies who belong on a leash. Either way, their fervent eyelash-batting could blow you back onto the streets. The unavailable ones, by the way, wouldn't belong to a club that would have you as a member, so don't even try it.

2 *To stir up some business.* The more obviously you do this, the more offensive you are and, therefore, the more business you'll generate. Don't just go out with an open mind hoping for the best. Actually think, "I'm going to make some contacts to-

---

● **The most grueling part of anyone's evening is waiting for afterhours clubs to open. Here (*left to right*) artist Russell Buckingham, club bouncer Mojo and "outlaw" party host Vito Bruno try to convince themselves that they wouldn't be better off at home.**

night." Then do whatever nastiness that requires.

3 *To have fun.* You're on your own.

Once you know why you're out, that'll determine who you associate with—photographers, journalists and celebs if you want publicity; nubile but not-too-attractive singles, pouting their lower lip and sneering their upper if you want a date; people with toupees if you want business; and none of the above if you're out to have fun—but there are rules. Here are the fifteen commandments of downtown, engraved on a guest-list clipboard and handed to the entire community from the rooftop of Danceteria.

1 Always say hello first. If you wait for them to say hello first, you'll be waiting all night and wasting the valuable time you could be using in saying hello to someone else. Your willingness to make the first step will both impress them and make them feel guilty. You can play on that guilt later and get at least one big favor out of them.

2 Never say, "What's new?" or "How are you?" These are the two most boring questions in the history of Western civilization. If people sense that you're going to ask either of those, they'll run in terror. Instead, try to subtly pump information out of the person you're talking to without revealing your own ignorance. Say, "Did you hear about what happened at Palladium?" then wait for them to tell you something that happened at Palladium.

3 Gush, but never drool. Drooling is aesthetically unpleasant and often requires dry cleaning. Gushing is sometimes messy, too, only do it if there's some truth behind it. If there's no way in the world you can gush truthfully, just nurse your drink and nod your head like one of those Buddha dolls in the back of cars.

4 Don't dish someone unless someone else dishes them first. Then make it

> • Diamonds are a girl's best friend, but any kind of costume jewelry—in fact, *all* kinds—are Pyramid Cocktail Lounge model/dancer/performer Gerard Little's lovers for life.

rhetorical, as in, "She's so tacky, isn't she?" Then pause as if you really want an answer.

5 **Make sure everything's off the record.** This applies to even the most insipid comments, as in, "This is off the record, but hi, what's your name?" Half the people at clubs are writing books.

6 **Work your own achievements cleverly into the conversation.** Say, "I love your dress. It reminds me of a painting I just did. Did I tell you I'm having a show at the Frank Bernaducci Gallery? Here's an invitation for the opening."

7 **If they're important, work the conversation back to the dress.** If they're not important, why are you talking to them in the first place?

8 **Wear high heels.** That way, you can see everyone there, and if someone rudely bumps into you, you can dig your heels into their feet until you spot blood.

9 **Don't ask anyone if they have drink tickets.** This will make all too obvious the fact that you don't.

10 **Don't fish for compliments.** It shows you're insecure. If they like something, they'll say it. If they don't, they'll say it too. If you sense they're about to insult you, change the conversation to how fabulous they look. They'll stop dead in their tracks.

11 **If someone fishes for a compliment, give it, but with such exaggerated enthusiasm they'll know you're totally insincere.** Say, "You look faaaabuloussss!" with a slight smirk that says I'm about to get sick and don't you dare make me have to lie again.

12 **Drop lots of names, but only if they're good ones and only if you have specifics.** Don't say, "I'm meeting Andy for lunch tomorrow," say, "I'm picking up Andy Warhol at twelve forty-five tomorrow and then we're going to have the veal special at Bar Lui, his treat." This will seem more truthful, even if it's a bald-faced lie.

13 **If you're spotted early, turn the accusation table around.** "What are *you* doing here so early?" Then turn the table back, say you're there so early "because it's so much nicer before all the trash gets here. I think less can be more, *n'est-ce pas?*" Again, rhetorical questions are the key, and if you can say it in French, even better.

14 **Never admit to not knowing something.** If someone says, "Did you hear Danceteria was going to be sold to Kathleen Turner's husband, Jay Weiss, but the deal didn't go through?" yawn and say, "Of course," even though it's the first you've heard of it.

But most all, don't be so preoccupied with rules. Be yourself. *N'est-ce pas?*

6

All Dressed Up with Everywhere to Go »

ever show your face unless it's properly painted—as these four British fashion perpetrators showed downtown in transatlantic-liaison Susanne Bartsch's "London in New York" fashion show at Limelight in '84.

Even when the lights go out on the Hassidic tributes and pornographic tone poems, there's plenty of entertainment to be had in downtown's most popular athletic event, people-watching. Some of the players in this sport look so flashy and attention-worthy clubs should pay them just for showing up—they're every bit as entertaining as any band they could hire and they're probably more musical. Some assemble their outfits with such shamelessness, they achieve staggering new heights of invention. Life, to these fashion outlaws, is one big modeling assignment, and anywhere they happen to end up is a potential runway. Feel free to point and ogle, just don't ask them what their philosophy of fashion is, or you'll be laughed not only out of the club but off the entire Eastern seaboard as we know it.

Their philosophy of fashion, silly, is that they don't have one. Creative anarchy reigns along with inspiration, mild insanity and personal style. If you have a strand of pearls, string it into your nostril or walk your friend with it like a dog on a leash—a true friend will let you do this for an entire night. Turn the classical obsession into wearable art (a tassled Eva Goodman dress featuring large Egyptian heads) . . . or make crass commercialism into fashion (lifesaver skirts, also by Goodman) and dubious patriotism into definite style (an American flag dress and shirt by Bayard that will guarantee a salute, or maybe a burning). These clothes are jokes on history, big business and other Trivial Pursuit categories, but can be construed as homages to the same, if need be.

Less is not necessarily considered more in this world where taste is purely subjective. The layered look is fine—designer Marc Jacobs says he'd love to wear twenty T-shirts and three jackets all at once. He's also had fun with polka dots, assaulting the viewer with dozens of big circles that seem to reproduce in front of your eyes. The same could be, in fact has been, done with stripes, cutouts and anything else that strikes the designer's fancy, preferably in bad taste.

Go for the impulse. If you have a nice hat, wear it upside down or inside out, or as a tie. How can you turn a hat into a tie? Well, as Joan Crawford said comfortingly to Christina, *"You figure it out!"* Figuring it out is half the fun anyway; the other half is getting oohed and ahhed over letting photographers think you'll make *them* famous if they shoot you—preferably with a camera, not a Magnum. While certain stars' bodyguards rough up photographers who take their picture, you should beat up the ones who *don't* shoot you. Son, you'll be asked who designed your outfit, and you can answer with pride: "Moi!"

Photographers are so exhibitionist crazy that anyone with a flair for assemblage can become a club star with a mere flick of the mascara brush. But while they're shooting you, you'd better come up with some bogus occupation you could tell them you excel in when it comes caption time. You should also think of a real occupation you could start excelling in—maybe temp work—fifteen minutes after the photo comes out.

In Kevin Boyce's case dressing up and getting noticed in the Studio 54 heyday actually led to a full-time career as a draping and runway model. That's not a typical profession for men outside the combustible world of nightlife. "I created a character to get into Studio, wearing thrift store dresses," says the cross-dressing son of a Philadelphia railroad worker. "The designers started to look at me because I was a man blatantly doing what I did, and they liked my sense of style and proportion. They started sending me couture clothes." On last count, Boyce had seventy-five couture outfits in his closet, all compliments of the designers.

Not only did they send him clothes but designers realized that this daring darling could be a perfect model for their most stylish women's wear. At 34–28–35 he had the same proportions as Margaret Donahoe, the country's top fitting model. And he had other qualifications.

"I'm very patient," says Boyce. "I could smack them in the face when they pin me. But I follow them. I have an instinct for the fabric. When they hand it to me, I know where it goes. One of the reasons the designers like working with me is because I look at it from both angles—women's and men's. I know what sells and what doesn't sell. I'd say I'm ninety-eight percent of the time correct."

His ultimate goal is to own a successful New York nightclub for chic people; in the meantime, he's having a great time being "more or less an event, a personality." He adds, "I've taken a large chunk out of life and had a ball. I did it all for fun. When it loses the fun, I'll stop doing it."

Boyce turned potential freak status into career magic and deserves to go down in fashion history for it. "This," he's quick to remind, "was before Boy George and before androgyny became trendy." Since then, of course, George made adrogynous a word even Middle America can pronounce. The rock star has been the greatest fashion motivation for downtown in the last five years or so. If someone could get away with that on nationwide television, shouldn't fashionplates in the underground scene be doing even more outrageous things? As he took more chances, scenemakers followed suit. He went further out into the sartorial stratospheres, and it became increasingly common to see men in items they no doubt claimed were birthday gifts for their girlfriends when they bought them. And as George came out with fresh, sharp and articulate remarks about everything from sex to . . . sexuality, it became more natural for people not to mince words, whether or not they were enunciated in a mincing way.

Meanwhile, the Eurythmics' Annie Lennox was giving her gender the chance to cross-dress, and Cyndi Lauper was taking the East Village style of incongruously assembled outfits of trash with flash into staggering heights of dementia. But while *People* magazine wrote, "Cyndi Lauper styles have caught on at Beulah Land (an art bar)," didn't anyone take into consideration the fact that the styles may very well have been at places like Beulah Land way before there was a Cyndi Lauper? A cable TV hostess who sent out press releases claiming Lauper ripped off her motifs helped fuel the flames of doubt.

"I'm always asked how culture is influenced by rock videos," says Lisa Robinson. "Actually, it's the other way around. Rock videos are watered down versions of what happens on the street." The clothes you see in New York clubs right now you'll see again in a couple of years when they make it onto MTV.

Fashion is the ultimate visual manifestation of the downtown attitude, a way to say whatever you want about yourself without having to use a single word. It's attention-grabbing—even if you aren't Somebody, you can become one by looking spectacularly imaginative. And peer pressure is so intense in the sartorial field that all those dressed just averagely look like complete slobs compared to the dazzling and disapproving hordes around them.

The most original downtowners are guided by what strikes them intrinsically as statements that will provoke a response, not by what Seventh Avenue dictates. There are enough survival problems—rent, jobs, relationships—to worry about. No one wants to feel regulated in fashion, too, when this is the one area there's no need for constraint in. There's no one telling you that you have to dress a certain way. If there's any pressure at all, it's to not dress boringly and to not follow what *WWD* says is in that Tuesday. Who wants to spend money on an outfit that'll be dated by Thursday? Better to get something individual and timeless that can be embellished and accessorized in dozens of different ways and last at least through the weekend.

Instead of slavishly recreating a trendy Western look, for example, as some London designers did, a better bet would be Andre Walker's tongue-in-cheek blend of Wild West and eighties couture. His chap skirt is tight at the hip and billows out above the knee, looking like something "Gunsmoke's" Miss Kitty would wear if she were going out clubhopping. Walker, who is a mere twenty, works out of his family's house in Brooklyn. He's influenced more by animals, furniture and lollipops than by fashion trends and is so resolutely unconventional he used his mother as the star model of his Fall 1985 show. Walker's success is partly due to the encouragement of Patricia Field, whose store on 8th Street has signaled trends and burst fashion bubbles for thirteen years.

"My philosophy of fashion?" says Field with a gasp. "I don't know. I don't get philosophical about that. It's out of my range. It's just personal taste, I guess, and education and feeling the vibes around you." Like Ellen

Stewart, who picks plays to produce at La Mama based largely on gut reaction (sometimes, reportedly, without even reading some of the scripts), Field hangs clothes in her store that move her. A barometer for downtown taste, she's been called the Geraldine Stutz of 8th Street. She knows that how to buy is the key to how to sell.

The vibes around Field's store are vibrant and offbeat, and not attributable to any one trend of the past few years (New Romantic, high tech, sixties, etc.), but the store combines all those trends, and none of them. In addition to the cowboy-and-Indian motif, there are psychedelic takeoffs, political T-shirts ("Dump Reagan") and everything but what's trendy. (Like the "Relax" shirts that were mass-marketed so that people could become walking billboards for a second-rate British rock band.) Field's clothes say "Relax," but don't spell it out.

True downtown style isn't force-fed like that, it comes out of someone like designer Michael Schmidt saying, "How about a link dress made out of shiny metal, heavy but worth its weight in drink tickets?" Or Pedro and Alejandro, downtown's designing Cheech and Chong, coming up with a look one model calls "Carnival in Nicaragua during a depression, but fabulous." Let J. C. Penney try to come up with that.

Large stores like Parachute and Unique Clothing Warehouse (which lives up to its name) offer the basic thrust of downtown fashion expressed in a more commercialized form— sleeker and more acceptable for those who want to cop a bit of the attitude without having to change their whole lifestyles. It's in the smaller shops, though, that the real statements are heard. The wide range of East Village boutiques can take you from the 1950s to the future, from Brazil to outer space, all with a rebellious spirit that translates into novel ways of assembling clothes. A store called Tribe has featured Alan Wilcox's silver oversized shirts with black crushed velvet sleeves while another store, Ona, has everything from "Rasta" hats to a sleeveless psychedelic dress to Lari Shox's doctor's jacket with painted-on planets.

Black Market sells only items in black—black leather voodoo teddy bears, for example—while Batislavia, run by two of Pat Field's favorite designers, Carmel Jonson and Pilar Limosner, has offered simple pieces that convert into more than one outfit and a Society for Modern Myths line of jackets and skirts inspired by cultural heroes from Gandhi to Liberace.

"I can't take fashion seriously," says Robert Molnar, who considers himself a downtown designer, even though his most recent showroom was located in the garment district. "There have to be other things to worry about. Why are people so concerned about matching shoes and bags and jewelry? I've actually heard women say, 'I can't wear blue because I had my skin tested and it's not on my color chart.' It's silly."

It's amazing that Molnar said that much. He tries not to talk about fashion at all, and also avoids fashion shows and *Vogue* magazine. He says that if he saw a Gaultier on the street, he probably wouldn't recognize it. More his style are see-through muumuus, ten-foot wigs and lamé jumpsuits, all of which come out of the fashion inspiration he got while apprenticing as a salesman at Sears. ("I thought Sears was high fashion," he laughs. "The first designer I ever heard of was Halston when he did ultrasuede luggage.")

Growing up in Detroit, Molnar started out in his father's not-very-fashionable plumbing business. "It was called T, M and B, which stood for Tony, Mary and Bob—and I was Bob. My father would teach me how to install water heaters in the projects. I thought, 'Oh God, this is my life.' Finally, I said, 'No, become an international businessman.' So, I went to community college thinking I'd move to New York and be like Bob Newhart on TV and live in a high rise and go to a businessman's club. I thought it would be so chic."

But even chicer, and more practical, was designing, which Molnar did without even the vaguest idea about color or seasons or right and wrong. That unique lack of restriction has led to what Molnar calls his Wing Ding look, a brutally funny slap in the face to anyone who slavishly follows fashion ins and outs. This line is so out it's very definitely in. The-look-no-one-wants-to-know-better, it glorifies white trash by making bellbottoms, leisure suits and hideously mismatched color schemes and accessories into a high-fashion assault that makes the wearer instantly popular, mostly because of sympathy. For anyone with the balls to wear it (and some do wear it without even knowing it), the Wing Ding look is the most fabulous trend for people who don't care about trends.

"Experimental and colorful—a lot of hand-painted stuff," is how Gloria Gabe of 109 St. Marks describes East Village fashion. Gabe and her husband came to New York from Milan and opened 109 in 1983 as a showcase for the work of local designers who sell exclusively in the store and through their wholesaling sideline. "So they grow with me" says Gabe. The shop, the first to give fashion shows at both Pyramid and 8 B.C., is flourishing in its timely location and has expanded to include its own small record label: 109 records feature the work of new young artists like Demetrious, who is also a model, and Killpig, who'll also presumably "grow" with Gabe.

Eva Goodman is one designer who sells colorful, offbeat work at 109. Goodman takes prints by artist Jonathan Bressler and embosses them in shiny rubber onto black ski pants, and does the same in black over white tank tops. She plays a lot with juxtaposition—of colors, textures and styles—and likes putting psychedelic motifs onto basic, form-fitting clothes. Her work looks like that of an '80s designer having a '60s acid flashback. One of her gold lamé jackets is half covered with paisleylike swirls, a visual treat from either side.

Designers who might be tired of having mega-department stores tell them they're too weird can settle into some stability at a store like 109—or, even more ambitiously, open a store of their own. Rather than sell to Macy's one year, to Bloomie's the next and to no one after that, designers can retail their clothes in loungelike boutiques of their own creation, where, if they fail, at least it's on their own terms. The entrepreneurial spirit is deep-set into the downtown consciousness. Why play along with big-business rules when you can make your own and still hold onto the dream that the big boys will not only notice you someday but ask you to name your price too. Then you won't be weird enough for them.

The shrewdest designers are the ones who scour the clubs in search of ideas to make their own, but their success depends on chance. The truly talented ones come up with the original concepts that make downtown fashion sparkle. Their clothes are actually worthwhile fashion investments, a rare commodity downtown. Getting a fashion-conscious East Village diehard to buy something off the rack is a major triumph when most can buy their own fabric and whip something together or puree some thrift shop rejects into a statement.

"My mother doesn't approve of the way I dress," says Anita Sarko, the queen of I-never-wear-anything-twice thrift shop chic. "She can't understand why I wear the clothes of dead people. I want to say, 'Then why did you tell me when I was fourteen to rat my hair and take me to a Vegas nightclub with no restrictions?' Only when I did radio interviews did she get excited . . . because she liked the way Barbara Walters looked." But Barbara Walters does not buy thrift.

Budget-consciousness is one of the main fashion inspirations on the scene. It forces you to make cheap look fabulous. Aware of this, many East Village boutiques are priced down to go with their location, giving the thrift shops a run for their discounts. These boutiques are that unusual concept, calculated commercial expressions of spontaneous style. They strive to be as zany and irreverent as possible, slickly turning studied chaos into an art form. Sometimes, the paintings on the wall seem as purposely crooked as the clothes are outrageous, but almost socially acceptable. These stores want to sell, not just to a few brave souls—"the walking wounded," as one Hamptons' newspaper condescendingly labeled them—but to a larger cross-section of New York society, the walking monied. Maybe as a result of their experiences with the department stores, designers are capable of accessibility as well as weirdness.

Julia Morton and Paul Monroe of Einstein's, which pioneered dresses for men, says a lot of their clients are middle-aged businessmen who find these unlikely gowns comfortable for lounging around the house: "But, Daddy, you're a drag queen!" Designer/entrepreneur Jo Dean finds that a lot of out-of-towners are interested in her look-at-me-I've-got-guts creations. (Out-of-

● Fashion goes round in circles, and so does boy wonder Marc Jacobs' polka dot line.

town, this look often reads as look-at-me-I've-got-a-death-wish.) Designer/painter Annie Waldrop used to make bizarre hats out of found objects and turn them into solar system bowlers, polar caps, coolie hats and piano key chapeaus. "But I wouldn't exactly say I was cashing in," she laughs. "They became decorations in my apartment.

"Now I'm working for a company in New Jersey, mass-producing hats and learning more about the technical side of designing and what it takes to make something that's saleable. However, it doesn't mean I'm going to give up some of my wilder ideas." She just might have to adapt them so they're more wearable, though. The old hats sometimes involved a kind of balancing act almost as treacherous as trying to succeed as a designer.

Katy K, a designer who's sold to big department stores and to country-western acts like the Judds and Rosanne Cash, has learned to perfect the same act. She started her own independent business after having trouble getting buyers to pick up on her square dance dresses and petticoats, though she did well with them at a seasonal Fiorucci concession. "I can't keep up with fashion," she says. "I'm not in fashion. People who like my style can come to me." Her style includes frilly, Nashville-inspired creations with lots of gingham and crinoline ("a sort of early sixties Kitty Wells look") that can be adapted to individual taste. "Whatever they want, I'll do," says the designer. "Some of it's pretty standard and some far out. I don't mind toning things down for one dress, but I hate doing it for a whole line, which is why I'm out of fashion."

And she isn't thrilled when she's asked to do the old Madonna look—all black with crosses hanging, "The complete opposite of me. I'm more into glamor and festivity. I hope that mole spreads all over her face."

Like Katy K, Keni Valenti opened his own business—the first boutique on Avenue B—"to make my own fashion and not be on any trend or color scheme. This is my shop and that's that." But also like Katy, he's toned down some of his wilder ideas, without eliminating the original effect in his repertoire. Having a store on the new frontier is "scary," he says. "Because it's not the neighborhood it should be yet. So it's a matter of sticking it out until it gets there." Meanwhile, he's benefiting from the five galleries in a one-block radius of his store—"All these artsy-fartsy people come in here"—and from all the East Village hype. However, he tries to separate himself from restrictive labels like "East Village designer." "There are so many of these kids and they're not really serious about designing. They're just trying to be trendy, and I don't want to be lumped in with it—I have nothing to do with this East Village look. Every day a new downtown designer is discovered. It's discouraging when I see these eighteen-year-old kids calling themselves designers and getting press in the *Eye*. I've been around for eight years and should be getting more respect."

Since he said that, Valenti's store *has* gotten more recognition for its diversity of outlandish and conventional things that neither local kids nor monied uptowners would sneer at. Valenti's a campy, hyperenergetic one-man show who says everyone should have a mother like his—she danced on "Hullabaloo" and had a twenty-inch waist and a new hair color every day. His favorite fashion exercise is to "wrap, tie and layer," removing all extraneous detailing so his designs are reduced to sculptural shapes. He works in mostly natural cottons, wools, silks and linens which he gets remnants of from local fabric stores and uses in clever and exotic ways. His Italian line, for example, consisted of monastic-looking suits and dresses in the colors of the Italian flag—red, white and green—adorned with the hand-sewn phrases "Italian #1" and "Made by Italians" and with hanging altar boys' tassled ropes. His "inverted L" cotton jersey dress is in a vivid variety of colors studded with row after row of black triangles. It hugs the body in bizarre ways, and is so lopsided FIT (Fashion Institute of Technology) had to design special hangers for it when they used it in a fashion show.

"I'm not just catering to the crazy people, who don't have any money anyway," says Valenti. "I'm catering to the art crowd, too. They'll buy the basic commercial things and the crazy things because they want to look like us, but they don't have the sense to buy thrift." They have the sense to buy Valenti. His "crazy" stuff is truly out there—seventies glitter rock outfits, overalls made from McDonald's and Rice Krispies bedsheets, eight-arm dresses, a wedding gown with a train that's a city-block long, a scarecrow line and a Gumbo Ya-Ya look based on Aunt Jemima. ("I hate it that every-

> • Designer Keni Valenti is now a "designer/businessman," having opened the first (but certainly not the last) boutique on Avenue B. His clothes range from sublimely outlandish to the type secretaries can get promotions in—satisfying a wide variety of tastes with all the trashy flash of someone whose mother danced on "Hullabaloo."

body always talks about London-London-London and Paris-Paris-Paris. America doesn't get the recognition it should. That's why I chose Aunt Jemima—an America icon. Who do we have to represent America? Calvin Klein? What bullshit.") His conservative stuff consists of more modified zaniness—streamlined, tasteful and understatedly overstated.

There's something in Valenti's store that'll appeal even to people with a forty-inch waist, one basic hair color and no dancing engagements except at neighbors' weddings. That's a diversity that's helped bring him from the realm of glorified fun and games into the world of serious business, a world where putting $500 down for a phone deposit is an important as finishing the new line. "I'm becoming this designer businessman," he says, putting two calls on hold. "I can't believe it!"

Similarly, as thousands pointed and laughed, Dianne Brill showed them what she was made of by becoming not only a designer businesswoman but a potential mass-appeal, super success story that no bra could handle. "I'll go really big," enthused the menswear designer shortly after Gary Bogard decided to back her work. "Bigger than I was. Lots of distribution and freedom to get the right fabric and ace production. The stuff will get all over the joint!" Brill is a woman of hyperbole that always turns out to be exactly on target.

Swathed in skintight rubber dresses, Dianne sometimes looks like a fabulously oversized latex glove. She's been romantically linked with Rudolf—in fact they're married but separated—and remembers how, after meticulously avoiding his advances, she realized he was devastatingly handsome and worth considerable trouble. "Probably I was not dressed properly in the Florida style," says Rudolf. "She was a totally new arrival and wanted someone with fast cars. Her dream was having a boyfriend with a real convertible. Even nowadays I don't have it." Maybe that explains why the relationship eventually cooled off a bit. But in any case, they're both still friendly and creatively aligned whenever the opportunity arises.

Brill is an ultra-ambitious ex-beach bunny who "used to have a surfer boyfriend and spent my days sitting on the shore in a bikini with a beach ball to watch him surf. It was so much fun." She grew up to design for such big-time surfer boys as Hall and Oates, Prince, Kid Creole and Adam Ant. When she did knockoffs, her logo was, "To the future through the past," but now her physique is as future-facing and all-encompassing as it looks. "I want to do everything," she says, looking quite capable of it. "I want to be a movie star without ever having to make a lot of movies. I want to be a huge designer. I want to go to big parties." She *has* to go to big parties; there's one in her honor practically every month.

The honor will expand as the work becomes more commercially practical, and Brill's shrewd enough to know that. Like the other designers, she's toned down her work. From her "Gumex" knockoff line she learned "how classically designed things can be redesigned into something modern." She also came up with the totally original line of New Millionaire's Club spring yachting wear—clothes that she says tend to emphasize all the right parts of a man's body. "It's not too weird," she says. "It's modern, free, sexy, body-flattering and more elegant than anything." All of those qualities plus the luster of trendiness, minus the intimidation of unbridled fashion statements, she hopes will prompt Mr. Middle America to reach into his best accessory, his wallet, and help spell out every designer's favorite word—success. Unfortunately, the press called Brill's August 1985 show "a fashion bust." The *New York Times* felt her yuppie clothes lacked personality. *New York Talk* said she was jumping on three-year-old trends with "gimmicky" dollar-bill sweaters and baggy pants.

Dianne Brill lacking personality? Has the queen of downtown gone uptown? Yes, but those distinctions hardly exist anymore as both up and down feed off each other in a mutually exploitive yet beneficial relationship. Brill has to span both realms. Even if she stood below 14th Street facing north, her chest and ambition would go well beyond that line of demarcation.

"It's about time everybody cashes in on what we've been doing," she says. "Why not? We've been busting our asses for a long time, and it's never crossed over. We had low rents and could be cool. But now we're paying a thousand dollars a month, and we have to be more materialistic. That's the way the world's turning. And we are ahead, so go for it. Fuck, cash in."

The biggest downtown fashion success story in recent memory belonged to Stephen Sprouse, who fused elements of sixties chic with eighties street smarts and took it to the top of the glitter barrel. It was far from a typical ascent. Sprouse didn't claw his way to the top the way most designers would like to. Rather he was discovered—much like those 1940s Hollywood actresses were supposedly "found" at Schwab's Drugstore. People just wanted the sparkle and style he had to offer. The ex-painter/photographer drew clothes as a nine-year-old from Indiana and actually made some several years later for a woman named Debbie Harry, who happened to live in his building. After dropping out of design school to work as a sketcher and fitter for Halston, Sprouse started his own design business in 1983—some say just so his friend Steven Meisel could photograph his clothes. At this point, though, the designer says, "Fashion was like a hobby for me. I never really trained." Success, he adds, "came almost by accident."

It also came quickly and grandly. He showed his festive day-glo and graffitied fashions in a Polaroid-sponsored young designers show and was discovered by Bergdorf Goodman and featured in *Vogue*, all less than a year after he'd started designing full time.

His clothes—day-glo minis in electric greens and oranges, colorful plaid and

● Stephen Sprouse's backwards-graffitied day-glo fashions were a huge hit in his SRO '84 show at the Ritz. But forwards, the writing on the vinyl spelled doom for the soon-to-be-bankrupt designer of '60s-chic-meets-'80s-street-smarts. A comeback is inevitable.

peace-sign-studded jackets—were both hip and glamorous fashion to shimmy in. Fashion commentator Walter S. commended Sprouse for "his ability to bring his favorite sixties shapes into the present by layering them with new proportions and signature accessories—engineer boots, name belts, Christian's knots, etc." Fashionplates rejoiced at the mingling of rock and fashion, the likes of which hadn't been seen in two decades. Other were not so impressed. "I have a *Harper's Bazaar* from the nineteen-sixties," says Keni Valenti, "and what he did is the same exact thing you find in there."

But Sprouse, thirty-two, never claimed to be terribly original. "I just take from people in the street and magazines," he said, so quietly you could barely hear him. (Sprouse is a man of many sequins, but few words.) "The street is where I get most inspired." Unlike Keith Haring, though, Sprouse didn't pick up on street style by hanging out with the hip-hop kids. He merely sat back and observed them from a shrewd distance. His items with numbers and letters scrawled backwards on them, he says, "were inspired by the kids who write all over their jackets" and who flawlessly coordinate outfits of studied casualness from their baseball caps all the way down to their all-important shoes. Sprouse's backwards-graffiti messages spelled out everything from rock lyrics to the Lord's Prayer—all in fluorescent colors.

The sixties inspired Sprouse so intensely because, "That was when fashion got to its most artistic point to me. They don't do it like that anymore." He sound like Lillian Gish waxing nostalgic about the silent era. Yet, at the same time, he says, "I like anything that's new—wilder or bolder, funny or dramatic." Sprouse's forte was something old made new. Like sixties nostalgia, his revamped retrospection appealed both to people who were there and to the intrigued who wished they were.

Sprouse's success, despite what some considered a minimum of originality, was easy to understand. Downtown can't get enough of the sixties and of sparkle. Those who lived through that decade remember it as a period of creative wildness and unmitigated openness and are continually trying to make sense out of what they grew up with, redefining it into relevant new statements. Those who are too young to have experienced the sixties firsthand have their ears burned by people rhapsodizing about it . . . hear strains of it in the music of Prince, the Eurythmics, Wham!, Sting and Aretha Franklin . . . and are fascinated with what sounds like a time of love-ins and Twiggy and civil rights protests and "Baby Love." (They never hear, conveniently, about the riots, assassinations and the less uplifting girl-group utterances like "Nothing but Heartaches.") Psychedelia runs particularly rampant in the nostalgia department. The idea of total mental abandon is very appealing, especially in a simulated retro context, where you only have to check your mind at the door until the theme party's over. Sprouse's controlled abandon fit fabulously into this milieu.

For a while, anyone who wanted a trend handed to them off-the-rack wore a Sprouse as if it were a second skin. The name alone was VIP room magic. If you told a doorman that your $3 thrift shop jacket was Sprouse, his eyes lit up with little neon bulbs that spelled out, "Come in, phuleeeze!" Then the designer's work became more widespread. You saw his sparkling things on omnipresent deb Cornelia Guest—talk about widespread—and some of the Guest list, a dubious fashion distinction indeed. Even Carol Channing, of all people, has worn Sprouse, telling *Vogue*, with her typically self-contradictory charm, that she loves his "alarming, screaming blues and neon greens," and that he's a designer of great dignity. Channing—the older generation's Teri Toye of Broadway—was so gung ho about her Sprouse collection, she proudly announced her intention to wear one of his flourescent green jackets to the Christian Science Mother Church in Boston. Maybe Limelight would have been more appropriate.

"I was ecstatic that someone was making black clothes that I liked," says media personality Lisa Robinson, an early supporter. "He was taking the excitement and energy of the past and bringing it up to date, making classic, tailored things for women. And the sequined and day-glo things were so much fun, though I never wore them."

Fun was what Sprouse's success was all about, but seemingly at the height of it, the strangest thing happened: He went bankrupt, and his family, who'd sunk nearly $1.5 million into his business, kissed it goodbye. Soon, leftover Sprouses were being auctioned off for the cost of a sequin. Even his office equipment was up for sale. The designer's seventies line of maxiskirts, bell-bottomed suits and wool jersey psychedelic print dresses and body suits never even made it to the stores.

What happened? Rumors had it that some of his clothes were less than perfectly made and had to be bargain-racked. Also, that rip-off artists were knocking off his glittering and graffitied items and selling them for far lower prices. But with sales of $300,000 in 1984 and about $500,000 in 1985, it's hard to fathom that factors like those could have hurt him much. Bad business management is what really did the designer in, leaving him with $600,000 of overdue bills.

Some observers say the seventies line that never surfaced showed a new side of Sprouse's talent, while others insist it was an obvious next step that proved he's little more than a clever rehasher. "Can't he do anything new?" says Albert Crudo, a young designer of tropically colored women's bathing suits and other kitschy but highly wearable flashwear. "He doesn't make fashion, he just repeats it like a bad Mexican dinner."

You can still see Sprouse's sixties stuff on anyone who hasn't renewed her *Vogue* subscription for two years, but chances are you won't see them anymore on model Teri Toye or photographer Meisel. Their Dynell Cleopatra wigs and know-it-all chic reportedly were major inspirations for the designer. (Toye starred in his breakthrough show at the Ritz, and Meisel supposedly had a hand in creating both of their career successes.) Now, when asked if Toye was an inspiration, Sprouse becomes a man of even fewer words. "No," he says, lowering his head. Case closed.

The group of Sprouse, Toye, Meisel and musician Richard Sohl—an airtight ensemble you could find in certain corners of any decent party just like you could always find your high school elite in the same nook of the cafeteria—splintered off in 1985, victimized by mutual resentments and backstabbing. "Groups of friends are normal," says someone who was sometimes part of this one, "to shield yourself from the big bad world out there." Normal? They were definitely fabulous (or at least they seemed to think so), yet few would label this group "normal," especially when you consider Toye's unlikely rise to modeling stardom.

Born on New Year's Eve and growing up the adopted son of an Iowa engineer, Toye moved to New York, attended fashion school and matter-of-factly became a girl. Shortly after that event, she was discovered as a model, winning gigs that ranged from Gaultier's New York show to classy Parisian stints. This development caused one wag to comment, "Only in New York could a boy from Des Moines become an international high-fashion model." Toye had the look—pasty, blond and ghoulishly intriguing—that made everyone think, "Someone that blasé has got to know something." Toye furthered her reputation as the blithe queen of outrage by having a party at Limelight to celebrate her mock engagement to Meisel and by climbing over the roped-off door area of the same club on another night, peeved that the doorman failed to recognize her. "But she's a fabulous personality," says the club's Fred Rothbell-Mista. "Fabulous personalities should do things like that. It's like Bette Midler saying, 'Fuck You!' on stage. If they don't do it, no one will." Unfortunately, in early 1985, *Vanity Fair* decided that Toye wasn't a fabulous personality anymore and that her fifteen minutes of fame were up. They also practically spelled out the fact that it was no one's loss. Shortly after that, she proved them wrong by modeling for Chanel.

Is Sprouse's time up? Probably not. He's vowed to come back with new support, and it's almost inevitable that he will. Still, there's a certain irony in his situation, which proves that even when downtown designers make it big, they may not have made it for good. At his peak "funny" is the word he used most often with regard to his success. "For the first year, I thought it was so funny," he once said, before the laughter died. "I was amazed. Now I know this is it."

7

"Come Up and See My Etchings... No Seriously"

A club with a bare wall is like a day without sunshine. So, Kamikaze became an art bar, serving up angst and Amaretto, and featuring a huge, imposing mural by Andres Garcia called, appropriately enough, *Kamikaze Lust*.

Art has become so part-and-parcel of the scene that it doesn't have to be in frames, or even in galleries anymore. At Palladium, it's everywhere you turn, from Keith Haring's overpopulated theatrical drop to Francesco Clemente's disturbing mural of wildlife gone amok. It's probably Jean Michel Basquiat's frescoes in the Mike Todd Room that echo the running theme of confusion with the most eloquence. "Eep, eep," his disembodied creatures and assorted skeleton heads are saying, but if you look at them in one of the room's twenty-nine mirrors, they're saying "Pee, pee." Either way, it seems terribly engaging or engagingly terrible. And as the patrons are torn between thinking it's meaningless garbage and knowing that it's widely celebrated and quite possibly a modern-day masterwork, you can almost hear them muttering to themselves in unison, "Eep, eep." As the club's co-manager, Ian Schrager, told *New York Magazine*, "It's like the emperor's new clothes. Who's going to say it's not good?"

"Jean Michel used to sleep on my floor," says John Lurie. "It turns out the reasons he made it had nothing to do with his talent. I shouldn't say that, it'll get him pissed off. But I mean it's more of a sociological phenomenon than anything else. I happen to think he's great."

Five years ago, Basquiat hardly had enough money to buy art supplies. He slept on friend's couches until he was thrown out of them one by one. But when the media leaped on him as the new art sensation, those same friends all but started asking him to autograph the sheets he slept on. His colorful canvases of primitive forms have put his work in the six-figure range and on the cover of the Sunday *New York Times Magazine*, where, barefoot and in a pinstripe suit, with his hair sticking up wildly, he was touted as the ultimate primitive at age twenty-five. But of course once a primitive makes the cover of *The Times*, he instantly becomes about as primitive as Stephen Sondheim.

Basquiat's story is typical of his time. The art market now is such that there's a constant craving for proverbial overnight sensations. No longer do artists work and live in the seclusion of the art world totally separated from public scrutiny. Now, the art scene is covered as if it were just another division of show biz, and has become far more integrated into the popular culture. People invest in art as they would in a lottery ticket—it's become a highbrow Wingo game. What's more, the pool of collectors has expanded to the point where they could fill a Haring mural, helping fuel this demand for "hot" properties. These collectors, often attracted by the trendiness of art more than any deep-rooted interest in the work, like to pick up on ascending artists while they're still downtown and more affordable. Once the artists have graduated to SoHo and then 57th Street, they're not only more mainstream, they're more expensive.

Basquiat filled the need for a new supernova quickly and well. The Brooklyn-born artist of Haitian and Puerto Rican descent first won notoriety as half of an anonymous duo of graffiti sloganeers scrawling intriguingly cryptic remarks like "Stop running with the radical chic playing art with daddy's dollars," in public places, attaching the tag "SAMO" to them. Ever the starmaker, dealer Mary Boone noticed Basquiat and gave him his first solo show in May of 1984. That same month, an exhibit at the opening of the renovated Museum of Modern Art featured a Basquiat self-portrait. It wasn't long before a painting of his, which originally sold for $4000, was auctioned off at Christie's for $20,900. His success was cemented, at least for that year.

Basquiat mixes comic book influences, voodoo, Caribbean mysticism, Picasso and absurdity, painting figures with eerie masklike faces studded with words, appliances and other side effects of a high-tech culture. "Nitty-gritty" is the adjective most used in connection with him because his works carry heavy emotional weight, especially when compared to the frivolous touch of many of his peers. (Next to the pop-arty assemblages of the Tweety Bird and Jetsons brigade, even "eep eep" seems to mean something).

Basquiat came a long way from the streets to the Boone Gallery, from selling one of his photocopied postcards to Andy Warhol for a dollar to becoming one of Warhol's protégés and collaborators. But now the same forces that hyped him to the stratospheres are wondering if there's more to Basquiat than sticky fingers and endless drive. Will the art buyers who buy his work the way you would a co-op find themselves with SAMO all over their faces?

"He'd do anything to get what he wanted," according to one ex-friend. "Every day he'd sit on Warhol's door hoping Andy would make him a star. That was fixed in his mind. I've never seen so much determination.

"I think he has a very loose mind. He can come up with statements and put them into symbols very quickly. He did a Pat Field window that was neat and disciplined. I didn't know he was capable of it. It was beautiful, not slapdash. I must say that despite all the bad feelings I have for him, he's very agile."

So agile, in fact, that she claims he never returned an accordion he borrowed from her when he started his band, Gray. "He's a user," she says, with a barely perceptible glimmer of admiration in her eyes.

A lot of people think Basquiat's gotten too big for his britches, but others disagree, insisting he was always that way. Keith Haring and Kenny Scharf, who remember him when he was a mere upstart, rush to his defense. "If I'm grouped with anybody," says Scharf, "I don't mind being grouped with Jean Michel and Keith. I always felt that we were together—not necessarily our art, but that we all came to

● Everyone converges around Jean Michel Basquiat's mural in Palladium's Mike Todd Room, and not just because it's behind the bar. The neo-primitive, voodoo-inspired artist of "nitty-gritty" works is the most celebrated and argued-about of recent art superstars.

the city and were friends when we were young. I always felt that we were the three main artists." His feeling wasn't just a wacky, self-indulgent notion. Soon, it was shared by many. Haring made it first, then Basquiat, leaving Scharf to freak out. "I was like, 'Uh-oh. I was there, too, and now they're going to leave me behind.' I wasn't going to let that happen."

"I met Jean Michel and Kenny in 1979," remembers Haring, completing the trendy triumvirate. "They were among the first people I met in New York and they're still my favorites." This mutual admiration society could make you mildly nauseous. But as the tightly connected Three Stooges of the Lower East Side, their rise-against-all-odds was smoother than it would have been solo. And now they're all secure, and different enough to bury any possible jealousies.

Haring, in particular, went from shy obscurity to total saturation with a vengeance, so much so that a lot of people felt they were being force-fed. Virtually every subway station seemed to have a Haring chalk picture. "The idea of my work being that quickly adapted into the culture is just what I was trying to do," he says in his large studio space while street kids you might not want to tangle with in a dark alley saunter in and out. These kids aren't only his friends, they're his inspiration. On the walls is the entire spectrum of the Haring saturation—a picture of Grace Jones bodypainted by him, a Warhol shot of the artist nude on the beach, a *Scholastic* magazine spread he did and a work that the artist simply calls "Debby Dick."

"Some people resent you the moment you sell a painting," he says, "but I don't care anymore. I realize what my priorities are."

Some of those at the top of his list are exposure, publicity and sales, which he executes with careful calculation. A couple of years ago, for example, he turned down a Bloomingdale's tie-in, because "I didn't want the whole thing to happen too quickly. I wanted things in the real world—murals, museums, galleries—so I'd be taken seriously, so I wouldn't be a flash in the pan." That's how a lasting achiever is made. As Warhol once said, "Business art is the step that comes after Art . . . and good business is the best art."

Haring arrived in New York from Kutztown, Pennsylvania, in 1978. An art student who read his neo-Dada poems at Club 57, his life changed in 1981 when he passed a subway corridor advertising placard that was covered over with black paper. As if struck by lightning right out of *Lust for Life*, he ran upstairs to buy chalk and came down to draw a flying saucer zapping a dog on the placard. Haring had gone from an abstract painter who did some cartooning on the side to a full-fledged graffiti artist incorporating his cartooning skills into every work.

With chalk and/or Crayolas ("50 cents, 30 pictures"), Haring brought art back into people's everyday lives, where it had never been in the first place. You couldn't help but stop and

notice his quickly rendered but rectilinear and neatly done radiating babies, dogs, snakes, atomic symbols and TV sets—but if you wondered what they were all about, he refused to spell it out in chalk or anything else. His whole purpose was to create a world into which limitless meanings could be read. "I don't think anything should be taken at face value," he says, adding only that his work is "both upbeat and satirical."

And what about those nebulous stick figures? Are they symbols of faceless man in the eighties? "They're just symbols of humans instead of actual personalities and can be any color or age group. It's the sign of a person—it can be any person or every person. The form or shape of a person instead of a particular person. It's a way of looking at the world—stylized instead of naturalistic."

Ironically, though Haring's written that the contemporary artist has a responsibility to continue celebrating humanity, his works seem icily impersonal. Those who want a more personal touch might appreciate a work he describes as "Mickey Mouse about to get fucked by E.T." But it's probably more constructive to wonder if Haring's graffiti work—like a featureless man being caught in a serpent's jaw—represents how "We're all getting swallowed up by some fuckin' snake," as one observer put it. Or maybe how we're all getting caught up in the art hype.

Whether you think Haring's work is just a lot of hot air on canvas or not, you have to agree that anyone who's transferred graffiti art into a lucrative enterprise is someone to scribble home about. With the help of dealer Tony Shafrazi (who first won notoriety when he defaced Picasso's *Guernica*), he's made the big step from being a vandal to having the kind of success that's inspired many artists to copy his style, the way kids used to study with that John Gnagy home kit.

Haring's a true eighties artist, as adept in his business dealings as he is in his art. He's so shrewd a self-promoter that when he printed twenty thousand

MICHAEL MUSTO

• A hard worker and tireless self-promoter, Keith Haring has brought his eye-grabbing stick figures of snakes, radioactive barking dogs and faceless people from the subway to the big league art world.

Nuclear Freeze March posters at his own expense, some said it was just another career move. But could they say the same of his more recent cause-obsessed, poster-style paintings that deal with AIDS, apartheid and the controversial death of Pyramid employee Michael Stewart? Maybe. Though he swears he's not a businessman, Haring has cleverly masterminded his ascent from the subways to the world of big business. In 1985 he designed the heart Brooke Shields held in her widely seen Richard Avedon-photographed poster. He also designed a Swatch wristwatch and mulled over offers to design computer programs and various other products. And, at the urging of Andy Warhol, he put together the inevitable next step—a store, in which he sells posters, shirts, buttons and basically himself. Some say this is an outrageous sellout—artists shouldn't mass-market their work in boutiques. Haring insists it's a generous act that makes his work accessible to the public at reasonable prices. It also helps him control his own merchandise and fight those counterfeiters who've turned up everywhere from Australia to Greece.

Despite his incredible publicity-willingness, the artist still comes off as remarkably unself-impressed. To this day, he keeps fit by doing street and subway work in between the pricey commissioned stuff. He says he'd rather hang out "with poor people" than celebrities. That's one reason why Haring's parties are unique New York events, combining the most exalted lowlife with the most glittering socialites—everyone feels part of Keith Haring's success. People from all rungs of the social ladder are drawn to his work, giving him just the kind of universal appeal he aspired to. And as trendy a success story as his has been, he's always kept his humble roots, mingling with hoi polloi as he sells to high society. That's the essence of the new downtown artist—an affinity for the streets that doesn't die even when those very street smarts take him to the penthouse level.

Kenny Scharf could have a party in his studio without even inviting anyone—his paintings and decorated rooms explode with enough characters to make up a long and very zany guest list. Originally, Scharf used actual characters from the Flintstones and the Jetsons in his work. "It's not my fault that Hanna/Barbera's in my unconscious from having grown up with it." But he's evolved into using his own characters, which are a hybrid of famous cartoon personalities but made far more goony and abstract. This not only gives his work more of an original stamp, it resolves potential legal problems.

Scharf's phantasmagoric landscapes, also represented by Shafrazi, have provoked more than one critic to remark that it's nothing more than trash peopled with grinning idiots running around what looks like "prom night on the IRT." "But I like a lot of trash," says the easygoing, but hardworking artist, "So, maybe it's not bad they say that."

Los Angeles-born, School of Visual Arts-trained Scharf, twenty-eight, had his first show at Fiorucci and says he totally expected his eventual success, which was cemented at the 1985 Whitney Museum Biennial—an exhibit presented by the Whitney curators that was to be a representation of the work of current American artists.

Scharf's contribution, an eye-assaulting day-glo corridor not unlike his Palladium Room, was easily the scene-stealer.

Two of Scharf's strongest memories of growing up are reading Time-Life books on Michelangelo and da Vinci and noticing that his grandparents had put plastic on all their furniture. Fortunately, they didn't laminate his art supplies. His influences range from pop art to Renaissance, and he managed to fuse the two with his version of Romulus and Remus with Jetson heads plus a Bellini Jesus surrounded by adorable Jetson angels. "Jetsons," says the (barely) grown-up space-age baby, "is nirvana."

When he got started doing his festive, disposable stuff at Club 57, Scharf says, "I didn't have any contact with the gallery scene. It was mostly just having fun—no one was worrying about their careers or galleries. We were actually against the idea of galleries. Well, now times have changed. If I were still a club artist, I don't know. I like what's happened. I'm able to do bigger things and make money, which helps." To cynics, Ronnie Cutrone's work, *The Love of Money*, might come to mind. "It's twue, it's weally twue," Tweety Bird is telling Sylvester, who's running through pasted-on dollar bills, "Money is the woot of all evil!"

But the money is well earned and

comes in more selectively now because Scharf only does paintings for shows, not on commission. He works, like Haring, without the least bit of preplanning. "I just start with my brush and whatever happens happens. It's more exciting for me that way. If I were to make a drawing before making it into a painting, I wouldn't want to complete it because I already did the drawing. I never like to repeat myself.

"This way, I feel like I can't make a mistake. I'm the one who makes the rules, so there are no mistakes. If I don't like something, I can just change it."

"Mistakes" haven't happened yet in Scharf's ascending career. His future, like Haring's, will bring him to an even wider audience with ever-widening pocketbooks. "I'd like to do mass-production kinds of things, like maybe making plastic toy monsters," he grins. "I've already made T-shirts and may do some rugs. But I don't know if I'd be able to work as easily with Brooke Shields as Keith did."

These new East Village-launched missiles have the benefit of what their predecessors have already learned in the commercial world. They're the second wave of eighties art stars, following hot on the heels of the much hyped SoHo artists who are by now entrenched in the highest art bracket, the same one the Harings and Scharfs are on the verge of. After a decade of dullness, the art world snapped back into shape in 1981 with the success of his first wave—Julian Schnabel, David Salle, Susan Rothenberg and others—self-conscious charmers, who were either the greatest thing since California rolls or nothing more than jokes perpetrated by the media—depending on your point of view.

The crucial aspect of their success is the way they were seized upon by art majordomos and nimbly marketed, much as the East Village wave would be later. That kind of manipulation proved just as important as the talent, which is still a subject of debate. Schnabel, for example, made his most critical advance when he won the support of the modern art world's two most influential dealers, Leo Castelli and Mary Boone, both of whom own SoHo galleries. Even when the Brooklyn-born, thirty-five-year-old artist was working as a cook, he fully believed he'd soon be New York's most celebrated artist, and told people so. These big-time manipulators helped him fulfill his dream, like Svengali hypnotizing Trilby, who in turn mesmerized the audience.

Influenced by European styles, Schnabel first attracted interest with his "plate paintings," which had pieces of ceramic crockery bonded to them. Some thought this crockery art was just a crock, but Mary Boone was intrigued. She brought collectors to Schnabel's studio and eventually gave the artist two shows.

The turning point was Leo Castelli also taking interest and agreeing to do a joint Schnabel show with Boone in 1981. Castelli, in his seventies, was eager to underline his place at the forefront with an artist he felt had char-

isma, both on and off canvas. This charisma was interpreted by others as bombast, especially when Schnabel told the *New York Times* that he considers his peers to be the artists who speak to him, namely, pretty impressive ones, like Giotto and van Gogh. That was Schnabel in a humble mood.

No matter, Schnabel's self-fulfilled prophecy was coming true as he headed for the stratosphere. In *New York Magazine*, writer Anthony Haden-Guest described Castelli's shrewd tactics in building up a reputation and high prices for his artist's work. Castelli selected five or six key collectors and gave them good deals. The collectors had excellent museum connections, which secured the possibility of the work being lent. Once the work was placed, the buzz went out with a vengeance. Then Castelli upped the prices, and that made other collectors feel they had to rush in before the prices went out of their reach. Schnabel had it made. Between 1979 and 1981, the price for one of his pieces jumped from $4500 to $15,000. By now, he can command up to $75,000, maybe more—though his profits will be shared by the Pace Gallery on 57th Street. In a highly publicized move, Schnabel left Castelli and Boone for an undisclosed sum (most speculators say it would have to have been well into and possibly beyond six figures)—that left no one in doubt of his ambition to continue his ascent to the top.

Meanwhile, New York was opening itself up to outside art influences like it hadn't done in a long time. Naples-born Francesco Clemente rode in with the Italian wave of neo-expressionists and was also shown by both Boone and Castelli (in separate shows), which secured his American status. His work has provoked a variety of adjectives from dark to unsettling to hallucina-

---

● A vision in day-glo, Kenny Scharf is as bright and kitschy as his own festively surreal, cartoon-influenced paintings. His controversial work is either transcendence or trash, but it's unquestionably made him a fluorescent success in SoHo, a long limo's ride from his disposable early work in influential performance spaces/hangouts like Club 57 in 1979.

tory to downright lurid. Critics have compared the work to the nightmarish fantasies of Bosch and Goya: most agree he's perverse, but wonderful. The most appropriate adjective, though, is successful. Clemente's asking prices at a 1985 Castelli show ranged from $35,000 to $90,000.

This unusually literate artist started writing poetry at age eight, and later studied Greek, Latin and Italian literature and philosophy. In 1973, two years after his first solo show in Rome, he started making nearly annual retreats to India, where he pursues the quiet Hindu life and paints.

The humble Hindus might be taken aback by Clemente's work, which deals in shocking juxtaposition. One drawing of his has a big, brooding character with two childish stick figures in its mouth and three lizards dangling from its hip. It's amazing that such a disturbing artist is represented at a major dance palace, Palladium, but today that kind of angst is part of the fun. And when he's not in Italy or India, Clemente is as integral to the scene as his work is.

Tour the East Village galleries and you'll see the seeds of future Clementes and Schnabels of the local variety. The Fun Gallery, where Scharf and Haring first came to real prominence, sparked the whole East Village art boom. An art party—a takeoff on pretentious SoHo galleries—is how co-owner Bill Stelling saw it. "I always had a lot of friends who were artists, so the Fun Gallery just happened," says actress/entrepreneur Patti Astor, who started the gallery with Stelling in July 1981 on a block that was a virtual cultural wasteland. "We were the first gallery in the East Village, and now there's dozens of them." Actually, Second Wave was the first, closing prematurely only because the esoteric owners feared it would become a big business (a cause for rejoicing, not fear, today). In any case, Fun was definitely a pioneer, and the first to last.

Their openings were true New York events with East Villagers gaping at this newly legitimized genre of art and street kids gaping at the limos lined up outside. Unfortunately, the graffiti craze proved to have limited museum appeal—and worse, Fun's biggest names like Scharf, Haring and Fab Five Freddy moved on to SoHo galleries, the inevitable next step for an ascending artist. That brought to light a built-in danger of the East Village art world: As long as it's the breeding ground for new talent, it'll have to wince a little every time an artist gets discovered and moves on.

But Fun could probably have gone on forever if it had been more deftly handled. Astor is said to have had as much business acumen as Sprouse. The Fun party ended in the summer of 1985, with Astor later holding a desperate auction to cover some of her debts.

The gallery, which Astor called "ultra-urban–contemporary," attracted widespread attention by showing the profuse but highly refined work of street artists like Keith Haring, Fab Five Freddy and Zephyr. "A lot of people who think of graffiti art just think of sloppy writing on the wall," says Astor. "We didn't really consider them graffiti artists—they're just artists—and people are always surprised at how beautiful their paintings are. They're very sophisticated and elegant."

All the artists "were people I knew who also had something to do with the club scene," she says. "Art creates the scene, and the scene creates the art. People who came off the street and expected me to go, 'Oh yes' to their portfolios were ridiculous. They should have started their own galleries and got their own scenes going."

Most of them have. The East Village art scene is so wide open now that seemingly anyone with the energy and a space—any space, no matter how creaky or unfinished—can become an art dealer. "I go to get something fixed at a hardware store," says one East Village resident, "and literally overnight, the store's been turned into an art gallery." And there's no lack of artists to show, either. All the people who wanted to be musicians in the late seventies now seem to be whittling their drumsticks into paint brushes. So, as a sheet metal place turns into a beef-processing warehouse turns into Vox Populi Gallery ("a masterpiece of carefully preserved decay," according to the *New York Times*), artists come out of the woodwork trying to pawn off their third-grade Show-and-Tell projects to the owner. Meanwhile, everyone else is furious, because they didn't think of it first.

"I only started selling paintings because I thought I wouldn't have to work for a living," says Vox Populi's owner Colin de Land, in all seriousness. "I thought I was going to ride around in limos, but it actually took me six months to sell my first painting." But that was uptown. On East 6th Street, de Land is finding that he can at least afford taxis.

Shrewd, eccentric, risk taking and dripping with charm that can turn sour when the need arises, the gallery owners may be the true stars of this burgeoning scene, but the artists themselves are hardly hurting from the opportunities it's presenting. "It's pretty easy to get a show," says Carlo McCormick, the *East Village Eye*'s twenty-four-year-old college dropout turned art critic. "That's the best thing about the East Village, more artists get a chance. But if you sit in a gallery for fifteen minutes, ten people will drop off their slides and you know they'll never get a show. They're losers—you can see it in their faces. For too many people, painting is a way of killing time. You don't have to justify your existence in society until you're thirty or thirty-five, so some people kill time with painting before settling into marriage or a job.

"It's even sadder to see forty- and fifty-year-old artists who are serious about painting, but who never made it in SoHo, coming to the East Village with their slides. Or some of the Club 57-period artists who never made it." Young or old, they're all so *eager*. *New York Magazine* reported that when New Math Gallery co-owner Nina Seigenfeld sprained her back and was being put on a stretcher, an artist came running up to her and said, "Is now a good time to show you my slides?" In the East Village, life is much stranger than fiction.

"The good art's getting better," says McCormick, but the bad art's getting worse. "The art boom is good in some ways," says Kenny Scharf, "but it also makes it harder to find the things that are really good. It seems like now, instead of going to art school, you just go to the East Village and have a show. I'm glad I'm not an East Village artist anymore. There are so many of them at each other's throats. It's so weird to think I had something to do with it all."

"It's vaguely amusing," laughs Keith Haring at the funny-strangeness of it all. "It's funny to me because of what it was like in the beginning—having these little shows in abandoned buildings and Club 57. From Patti Astor opening one gallery to dozens or hundreds—I don't know which—opening is amazing. But there's still not more happening artwise than before. More of it's getting seen, which is good, but eventually you hear about everything that's new anyway, and still only a select few stand out." In other words, more doesn't mean better. Just more. And the Fun Gallery closing might signal the fact that the boom has already peaked.

Stephen Style, who owns Sensory Evolution Gallery, was canned from his job as an art director for a lithography company. So, he blithely opened the gallery because his unemployment had run out. Sensory Evolution, which specializes in contemporary pop full of colorful, fun, figurative imagery, is just one of many alternative galleries in the neighborhood. The East Village "is the place for art right now," says Style. "Prices are a lot lower than SoHo, and the work is more on the cutting edge. It's not comfortable designer work, like a lot of the stuff in SoHo which fits in so well with the design of your house, you can buy it with a couch. Our art is more exciting than that." Ironically, though Sensory Evolution was one of the first ten galleries in the neighborhood and helped start the boom, Style had to find another space when the rent suddenly zoomed. One art dealer jokingly commented that rents are ris-

● The john at a funky but unfortunately defunct Alphabetland performance space called 8 B.C. became a minimuseum thanks to the mural painted by Rhonda Zwillinger (*second from left*), adding to the legend of bathrooms being the most happening part of clubs' layouts. She's joined by art dealer Gracie Mansion (*second from right*) and 8 B.C. co-owners Dennis Gattra (*left*) and Cornelius Conboy.

ing so quickly that in order to be an East Village artist nowadays, you have to commute from SoHo. Style, appropriately enough, has opened a SoHo branch too.

"I think it's kind of a joke in a way," says Cookie Mueller, *Details'* art critic, about the downtown art explosion. "There are a lot of galleries that are valid, but there are a lot that are crap. It's like going to the grocery store. Maybe I'm getting old, but it's become a real fast-paced business. It's like some discount retail outlet—art reduced by twenty percent. If it's not selling, slash it down. Art's all about money now. People can't afford real estate anymore, and they don't like jewelry, so they invest in art."

She looks chagrined, an emotion she perfected as an actress in several John Waters (of *Pink Flamingos* fame) films. "I don't know. Too many East Village galleries show nothing but arts and crafts."

Gracie Mansion is one gallery Mueller puts out all her most sardonic emotions for. "Welcome to the art supermarket!" is her succinct critique. Gracie's the gallery that's so controversial half the people you ask will wax euphoric over it while the other half tell you they're unavailable for the next year and slam down their phones. It's been celebrated, criticized, revered, debated over and always populated with people looking to see what it's up to next.

Mueller's not Gracie's only critic. "She sells art by the square inch," gripes one art writer, and Carlo McCormick adds that "Gracie's been slightly sucked into her media image."

But would any of Gracie Mansion's critics miss one of her openings? Even if the work exhibited there compels you to barf, at least it compels you. "And Gracie's energetic, loves her artists and cares about them, and is a master promoter," according to Timothy Greenfield-Sanders, who's photographed her and other art movers and shakers.

Gracie (real name Joanne Mayhew-Young) was one of the first to emphasize the smaller, more flexible and personal aspects of a gallery space, generally helping to make art shopping a little less of a color-by-numbers experience. Gracie explains that amidst the white, flat walls and spotlighting uptown, paintings are more likely to provoke reactions like, "Oh yes, Doris, this is definitely good." But in a gallery like hers, "People really have to be able to look at the artwork and know its value apart from the space. It's kind of funky down here."

The gallery is one of many downtown ones to attract a whole new breed of collectors—not the museums and wealthy big-timers so much as upwardly mobile young couples with a cultural craving. In fact, artists like Rodney Alan Greenblat often work with Gracie to deliberately keep their prices down to remain available to real people rather than twilight-zone people, or worse, no people.

Not surprisingly, Gracie started the gallery largely as a reaction against that horrible demon—SoHo. "SoHo had gotten to the point where it was nearly impossible for new artists to break in," says the thirty-nine-year-old dealer. "And all the artists I knew were doing work that I thought was a lot more interesting than what I saw in SoHo." So, like Sir Edmund Hillary, who climbed Mount Everest because it was there, Gracie opened a gallery because she could. A Pittsburgh native, Gracie first exhibited art on her bathroom wall: "A comment on the Lower East Side," she says, meaning that before there were galleries in that area, art popped up, by necessity, in the strangest places. Rather than flush the art, she decided to belatedly graduate as an art major from Montclair State in New Jersey (after a ten-year hiatus from college), then open a gallery with a partner, Sur Rodney (Sur), in which to show it. The gallery caught on, moved to larger quarters, and even spawned the Gracie Mansion Museum Store, where at one point you could buy champagne glass collages (minus the champagne) for about $100 and just plain glass accessories (minus the inflated price tag) for $7.

The gallery's art, on the other hand, has sold for as much as $10,000 a painting in the case of David Wojnarovicz's work, but Holly Solomon of East 10th Street says she doesn't pick art based on commercial considerations. "I look for artists who really take chances, who make some kind of statement no one else is making. It's not a particular type of artist I'm looking for. The work has just got to hit me on an emotional, intuitive level."

Walk into the gallery one day and you're not just hit, you're clobbered in the most enjoyable way. You might enter through cellophane streamers and see a whole self-centered art universe that only requires a willing suspension of belief in the real world to appreciate. Even the floor is part of it; it's been transformed into a turquoise sea, hopping with friendly fish and bathers, adding to the total experience of artist David Sandlin's satirical vision called *Religious, Mythological and Historical Art for the New Right.* Sandlin's primary influences seem to be fifties safe-driving commercials, game shows and B-movies like *The Creature from the Black Lagoon.* His paintings don't just illustrate slices of life, they all but talk to you with their billboardlike slogans.

One painting, ominously labeled *The Lord Wants to Help You*, features the most insipidly pleasant suburban woman saying to her husband, "Look dear, the fridge, the summer house, the vacation paradise. . . . Everything we prayed for." You soon realize that that green sea around you is the sea of American consumerism, and you'd better keep moving or you might drown in it. And just when you thought it was safe to go back to the galleries.

It doesn't take Siggy Freud to figure that for the East Village artist, kitsch is a reaction against the gritty reality of street life. "When you're so close to the street," says artist Hedy Klineman, who lives on Park Avenue, "you either portray the street or get away from it." Klineman's work includes assemblages of people's clothing and belongings which she transforms into highly personalized portraits, like the one of

Dianne Brill's bras wrapped around extra-large falsies. "East Village artists are on the ground floor, so their work is more about the horrors, suspicions, sadness and pain of urban living." Or, conversely, about the Flintstones, the circus and the American dream, with revolving amusement-parklike parts and bright, comic strip colors.

Generally, the work at Gracie, and most of the East Village galleries, veers wildly between those two extremes: junk-culture-inspired kitsch and ultra-heavy nuclear age angst. It's a strange dichotomy that mirrors that of the entire neighborhood—bright lights and razzle-dazzle mixed with rubble and heartache. It's not that hard to see the entire East Village as one big gallery, changing its surface about every month and swinging uncomfortably between satirical fun and games and paranoia, both real and imagined.

Most of the artists, whether perky or depressed, strive to be "read" fairly easily. "East Village art was always meant to be somewhat appealing and not that obscure," says Carlo McCormick. "Even though some of the artists would be abrasive to people, they like their work to be both artistic and understood. The avant-garde before that was belligerent. You had to sneer at the bourgeoisie—put a urinal in a gallery and make them cringe." Now, a color TV set redone into an art piece might be more like it. You don't want to spit in the face of the bourgeoisie when you secretly aspire to be them. Well, all right, go ahead and spit, but then clean it off and apologize.

There's still some good nasty art coming out of the scene. Michael Cockrill and Judge Hughes' *Win a Date with Brooks*, a sort of carnival-game painting, clearly makes fun of Brooke Shields and American iconography, but those are easy targets and it does so in a cartoonish, undemanding way. The work features a Shields lookalike's derriere, barely covered by black lace panties, jutting out of the canvas above the promise that "$1.00 Includes Snapshot." It's a like a *People* magazine cover come to life with wit, and an unwitting swipe at Keith Haring's commercial and unquestioning work with Brooke. Cockrill and Hughes also did a posterlike celebration of fellatio called, simply, *Suck*, which one critic wrote expresses the message: "You suck, art sucks, the whole world sucks." The downtown crowd would tend to suck in their cheeks and disagree, but enjoy. It is not boring.

Right now, most artists would prefer to think there's plenty in the world that doesn't "suck," especially the possibility of their own success. Tomorrow's art boldfaces are peering out of every East Village street corner, lurking behind every empty spray can. They're all competing in this desperately silly sweepstakes, and the winners could be anyone who happens to strike the right cord at the right time, thanks to crafty self-promotion and maybe a little talent, too.

Everyone in the know is placing bets on his own favorites. Some vote for Michigan-born, Chicago Art Institute and Pratt-educated Greer Lankton, who makes jointed doll-like sculptures out of wire hinges, fabric and glass—and they're not darling little Barbies, either. Klaus Barbie is more like it. Lankton's propensity runs more towards darling hermaphrodite dolls in labor, endearing repulsive fat-lady dolls and lithe and lovely Teri Toye dolls. They're uncannily lifelike, more because of the inner life they project through sheer visual impact than out of any naturalistic touches. They transmute the coyness of childhood playthings into something that's not only cuddly, it's almost savage. A Lankton doll is more likely to be wearing stigmata than beads.

Others vote for Stefano Castronovo, who made a name for himself by painting two gigantic Mona Lisas, one on a building in SoHo and one in the East Village, and inscribing his name alongside them in huge, impossible-to-ignore letters. Of course, this kind of bid for attention doesn't always result in career nirvana (and as Judy Holliday learned in *It Should Happen to You*, it shouldn't always happen to everyone). However, Stefano's managed to parlay his knack for self-promotion into a full-fledged career. Now, he paints pop images from Monroe to Presley to Fidel Castro on the back of leather jackets— a venture that's been so successful, he was able to jack up his price from $2000 to $4000 in just a couple of months. (That price, by the way, doesn't include the price of the jacket.) Warhol would be proud. In fact, he is, having already bought several of the artist's jackets with another famous pop image painted on them—himself.

Stefano's self-propelled, Mary Boone-less rise has been impressive, an inspiration for anyone with a paint brush, a blank building to use it on and the nerve to ask permission. The biggest money right now, though, is on two artists—Rodney Alan Greenblat and David Wojnarovicz—whose stars are rising so quickly they might soon join the gallery of pop images Stefano paints on jackets. No two artists could be more different, Greenblat with his fanciful universe full of amusement-park festiveness and Wojnarovicz with his tense commentary and jagged urban edge. But even if they're coming from opposite ends of the emotional spectrum, both have sparked enough comment and controversy to become the subjects of equal amounts of art-community hope (i.e. pressure).

"Wojnarovicz's one of the people who will last," says the *Eye*'s Leonard Abrams. "He can communicate the terror, tension and reality of living in the city, particularly if you're not well taken care of." The artist's *Science Lesson*, seen at the Whitney Biennial, is a barren earthly landscape, as seen from the moon, which shows our planet's terrain, possibly in the wake of a holocaust, surrounded by human debris along with free-floating houses, cows, planes and other memorabilia. Not very cute. But at the same show was Greenblat's *Ark of Triumph*, a piece with a life of its own (literally—it moves), filled with bright colorful cartoonlike figures, lists of famous names . . . from Walt Disney to Gertrude Stein to Mary Tyler Moore . . . and of

- **Valley of the Dolls:** Artist Greer Lankton (*right*) turned model Teri Toye into a playful work of art—the most blasé doll ever made. Few little girls would want to cuddle the Toye toy, but East Village galleries adorned their walls with it, and the plaything was last seen in the window display of Einstein's boutique. Teri, by the way, is smiling.

professions . . . "Lawyer," "Philosopher" and "Teacher" . . . all of which rotated under the prevailing theme conveniently written out for those who like a prevailing theme—"No more preconceptions." Great, but what does it mean? Maybe that all of those names, professions and even idiotic characters should be celebrated equally for their own particular triumphs. A message that left you feeling as buoyant as Wojnarovicz's made you queasy.

Rumor has it that Greenblat's parents forced him to go to amusement parks as a child—he was hard-pressed to have fun-fun-fun. "I watched cartoons my whole life," he says, "and I couldn't help incorporating them into my art, having sat in front of the TV for all those years. Now, I have a whole cast of my own characters." Greenblat has created an entire nameless world, "A place where anything can happen, and every day it's different. A world where they didn't have evolution. Everything's all there at once. It's kind of like being born—everything's there already. It's a retreat, but it's an allegory, too—for the real world. Bad things happen in this other world, too."

In the never-never land of art, though, Greenblat's well taken care of. Gracie Mansion has supported him with all the zeal she brings to her favorite pet projects. "He's said more about the American dream than I can hope to explain," wrote Mansion in an invitation for Greenblat's "The New World" show. "It's about a marriage of myth and reality, with a promise of a future filled with brightly colored houses." Co-ops, no doubt.

Kenny Scharf's opinion of Greenblat? "People are always asking me if he's copying me. But his work is very careful. Everything seems very thought out. It's fun art. It's nice to see fun art. I don't have to be the only fun artist."

That sounds vaguely secure, and angsty artists like Wojnarovicz, by steering clear of the "fun" category, are helping keep it that way. No one looks at Wojnarovicz's work and wants to start singing songs from *Mary Poppins*. "Some people look at my work," he says, "and it doesn't faze them at all. Other people are disturbed by it. Some people think it's not intellectual enough, or that it's too simple." Some, he adds in this rundown of his own critics, think he doesn't even know how to paint. But who said you had to know how to paint? The ability to disturb and provoke and even irritate is far more important, and he's got that market cornered.

Wojnarovicz's rise, achieved without formal training, has been as unorthodox as any in the Lower East Side free-for-all. As a member of the band 3 Teens Kill 4, he experimented with tape recorder songs—taping street sounds, West Side fights and other real-life situations that don't usually work their way into live music and mixing it into the set. "Some of our songs had no lyrics at all, just tape recordings," he says. He had no musical training either.

The self-appointed poster maker for the band, Wojnarovicz used stencils and spray paint, but found that people who didn't like the band—or maybe who did—ripped them down. His next step was not unlike Stefano's appropriation of open space. He just did it on a smaller scale. "I'd start spraying on walls and on abandoned cars. I also did stencils of burning houses on a gallery door. I had no intention of getting a show. It was just a reaction to my feeling that the art scene wasn't looking at new stuff. Right around that time, things were changing."

The Milliken Gallery approached him, and another gallery later put him in a show with Haring and Basquiat. While Greenblat's "brightly colored houses" were becoming valuable real estate, Wojnarovicz's burning ones were raging, too. But the artist sounds like someone more interested in learning and growing than seizing the spotlight, a rare point of view nowadays. "I don't trust my success. As easily as they give it to you, they can take it away. After a year they're bored and need something else. There's no patience for growth. I think it's safer not to spotlight attention because it'll last longer."

So, at the height of his popularity so far, Wojnarovicz is striving to make his work "more complex, more strong, less easy to read." He also took the summer off to drive across country and write. "I also take pictures and do small films. I can't imagine painting for the rest of my life. I want to step away from it and do other things."

Of course, for every inch he and others like him step away from it, there's a swarm of young hopefuls, canvases in tow, waiting to tap-dance their way in.

8

Curtain Up . . . Where Are the Lights?»

Beauty and the Beast," screamed the *Details* magazine caption, and Miss Hapi Phace (Mark Phredd, *left*) still thinks they were referring to him as the beauty. Miss. Tangela (*right*), aka Alan Robinson, knows better. The two are among the dozens of downtown drag artists who won't go on stage unless they're wearing just the right amount of mascara—much too much.

Virtually all downtown performers of any merit have passed through the stage of the Pyramid Cocktail Lounge, where they can try out wild ideas they previously could only fantasize about, applauding themselves in their own living room mirrors. At the Pyramid, they have the chance to dare and the honor of falling on their faces. It's a free-for-all showcase of talent so wicked and extreme it's the closest thing to a Berlin cabaret New York (or Berlin) has to offer and would fit very well into a number of Bob Fosse musicals. There's something eerily decadent about the obsession with drag performers who'll probably never be on game shows or on Broadway imitating those genres with a wide-eyed admiration that easily overwhelms their satirical bite. While the Mudd Club crowd aggressively deflated cultural absurdities, the Pyramid bunch embraces them. When they do a disco song, you get the feeling that they secretly always wanted to be Vicki Sue Robinson, even though they're usually playing it for laughs. They're willing to do anything for a laugh, and they'll also laugh at anything. Most of all, though, they'd like to be serious stars.

At the Pyramid, entire religious sects are formed around such exalted objects as "Gilligan's Island," Douglas Sirk melodramas, Disney cartoons and "People's Court." An evening's entertainment here might include a screwball version of "Family Feud," with John Kelly as Jackie Kennedy Onassis announcing, "We are not here for the money of it, we are here for the thrill of it," and answering questions like, "Name a place where people get impatient" (the hairdresser's, of course). Or "Vulcan Death Grip," Ann Magnuson's heavy metal-band takeoff, replete with skintight spandex and all the clichéd poses, inane patter and canned arena-style applause. The show specializes in songs like "Holiday in Hell" ("Holiday in hell and I'm wasted / I'm drinking all the piss and I'm wasted") and "Eat Shit and Die," a singalong during which the audience is urged to follow the bouncing skulls. "We played it backwards," Magnuson tells the audience, "and you know what it said? 'Kick ass, you shitheads!'"

The next night, the Pyramid will take you from Madison Square Garden to the MGM Grand, where John Sex—he of the gigantic . . . hair—performs his version of a Vegas lounge lizard with the shameless exhibitionism that comes from years of taking off his clothes in public. He's still doing a takeoff, but this time the clothes are on, and so's John, who emotes and postures through his own rendition of "That's Life" ("I've been a hustler, a hooker, a honcho, a hero, a dyke and a queen"). Then he tops that with his self-indulgent masterpiece, "My Face for the World to See," a collection of every cliché ever perpetrated by paunchy-but-vain Vegas crooners, during which he adores himself so fervently he practically risks death by autoerotic asphyxiation. Sex (which he insists is an Americanized version of his real name, Sexton) takes all the wind out of Liberace and Wayne Newton types. But don't kid yourself—if asked, he'd open for them in a second. *His* opening act, by the way, might have been Freida, a six-foot dancing doll—oh, all right, a five-foot idiot with a big doll head on top—turning the "Hail Mary" into a hilarious disco rap. Or Vaudevillia, a poet/singer who dresses in an evening gown with a rubber knife strapped on and does an elaborate act with smaller dolls. Or something more run-of-the-mill like an act called "I am a Japanese Jesus" (don't ask).

Sex, a former painter who says he couldn't effectively communicate what he thought onto a canvas, has no trouble doing it with a microphone, a neon-studded backdrop and a throng of people screaming "We love you!" A natural showman, the Long Island-born cheesebomb danced the Twist so hard when he was seven, his parents almost had to rush him to the hospital. He suppressed his theatrical side though, devoting his adolescence to trying to fit in with "the jocks, the hippies, the drug kids and the greasers" at high school. A few years later, among the stars, prima donnas, divas and deviates at Club 57, he finally found true nirvana. Just one go-go stint there, and suddenly John wouldn't get off the stage.

"I was hooked. I thought I was a star. I really thought that was the big time because all the girls went on and on about it. Of course, we got five or ten dollars a show." That paid cab fare home—and Sex lived across the street.

Like the strippers in *Gypsy*, Sex knew you gotta get a gimmick. So, he kept his catchy new surname (actually coined by two friends, Joey Arias and Klaus Nomi, not an Americanization of anything) and developed a self-mocking, larger-than-life bump-and-grind routine that was so much fun it clouded you to the fact that Arnold Schwarzenegger (or even Lisa Lyon) he wasn't. But he was kooky, and at least he had more sex appeal than those neatly coiffed slabs of Chippendales' ground chuck. "I've been to strip shows where the guys were too serious," says Sex, "and it didn't do it for me. I'm into bad taste. I think of Chuck Barris as a genius. Camp doesn't connote anything bad to me." He beams deliriously. "Camp is my life!"

But stripping is no longer his life, just an occasional hobby. Sex has revamped his act into more of a tribute to Jack Jones and Harry Belafonte than Jack Wrangler and Harry Reems, and it's worked. His erect hair and twelve-foot-long pet snake have been featured in *People* and *Us* magazines, and he actually got to record a four-song E.P. for Sire Records (featuring the single, "Hustle with My Muscle"), produced by top d.j./mixers Mark Kamins (of Madonna, Dominatrix and Cheyne fame) and Ivan Ivan. "We got the deal based on my personality," says Sex, "and the idea that those guys were going to produce it."

The deal could represent the next step—a national tour—for Sex, who's been working his adorable tush off on club stages for years and is now almost as tasteless and funny as the *real* Wayne Newton. "I'm not tired of playing the club scene. I get tired of not making enough money. But I'm happy. I just want to be up there. I want everybody to like me." It's easy to like John. More people than ever want to get near his snake. Even more want to massage his irresistably stiff hairdo—even though they know that since he keeps it up with a mixture of Dippity-do, Aqua Net, beer, egg whites, and semen, among other things, it would be far from safe.

The Sex name is indeed starting to develop that certain ring of celebrity. "Except," he laughs, "when I make business calls and say, 'This is John Sex,' secretaries get nervous and give me the runaround. They think I'm a crank caller."

The Pyramid is smoky, dirty, narrow, crowded and totally fabulous. One club that's managed to avoid a certain snob appeal—something that can spell quick death once the snobs decide to go somewhere else—it's preferred to keep the emphasis on disposable fun rather than fashion and pretense. If there's any problem with it, it's the same one that plagued and ultimately dissolved Club 57—the shows and performers that work out the best are the ones that are continually brought back while the less sure things are often left out of the running. As a result, the Pyramid stable of stars, like Louis B. Mayer's in the thirties, sometimes seems like a suffocating clique no matter how fabulous they are.

And though he says the club's been a great showcase for his work, writer Mark Oates adds, "It's also disposable. Three-and-a-half years later and nothing has come out of there. An evening's entertainment, and nothing's stayed or developed. John Jesurun did the most critically acclaimed project [his forty-four-part 'living film serial,' *Chang in a Void Moon*], which took him to La Mama and Europe. But most things are temporary and aren't given real care. Of course, that's part of the charm of the place, too—but now, if I want any kind of lasting career, I move on."

The club was originally a blue-collar bar, where the chief attraction on a good day was three fat Ukrainians guzzling beer. No wonder they welcomed former Interferon manager Bobby Bradley and ex-Mudd Club doorman Brian Butterick's idea of doing a downtown party there in December 1981. The astounding success of that evening led to Bradley's regular gig there, and after a month and a half, even the *New York Times* had picked up on it. Soon limos were lining up on Avenue A in hopes of seeing the latest entertainment outrage, not to mention the drag queens dancing on top of the bar, certainly more of an attraction than those three Ukrainians.

Meanwhile, performers like show biz vet Chi Chi Valenti brought their own house slippers and a roll of toilet paper—"the star treatment." And Benjamin Liu—Andy Warhol's assistant by day who doubles as drag lip-sync performer Ming Vauze by night—would go from receiving audience worship to relieving himself behind a pole in the back because of a distinct lack of facilities ("Very glamorous," he laughs). Somehow though, it *was* perversely glamorous, and the facilities eventually were improved.

"The Pyramid is totally unafraid," said publicist Susan Martin, even after she was let go as the club's flack when they made budgetary cutbacks. "It's the most iconoclastic, wacky, tacky, irreverent place in town." Since saying that, she was brought back.

Oates, who wrote the club's amusing and strangely poetic *Psycho III—The Musical*, says he likes it because, "The people there know the words to every TV show theme. The true Pyramid—and downtown—person finds humor in everything. Ann Magnuson said about satire that it's like nuclear war—nothing is spared. That's kind of the downtown sensibility—mirroring authority and laughing at it at the same time."

At the Pyramid, Oates says, "It's really kind of a Judy Garland-Mickey Rooney 'Let's put on a show' spirit. You don't need a million dollars to put on thirty minutes of good entertainment." Oates only needed about $2000 to do the video for *Psycho III*, something he should win a special downtown Emmy for, but he deserves nothing short of the Pulitzer and the Jean Hersholt Humanitarian award for putting the actual stage show together for considerably less—$100. That, by the way, didn't include a publicity budget, so Oates found himself glamorously involved in pasting and sticking, something Mike Nichols hasn't been seen doing in some time.

"If you perform in a place like Pyramid," says John Kelly, "you can perform anywhere else. I've learned a lot about engaging an audience, letting them know you want them to get it. They're right in front of you, so there's no way you're not going to get involved with them, and vice versa." Kelly's a professional dancer who apprenticed with American Ballet Theater, but he quit dancing eight years ago to study fashion illustration. "Now, I just put all that stuff together and approach it as a visual artist and not a cabaret artist." Oh, he sings opera, too, and also does drag characters like Dagmar Onassis, "the illegitimate daughter of Aristotle Onassis and Maria Callas," who has yet to be asked on "Family Feud."

It's an impressive list of credits, but hardly suprising. Few downtowners, after all, have a talent. Most, like Kelly, have several. Pyramid favorites Mark Phredd and Stephen Tashjian are also artists. Kenny Scharf directed videos, gallery owner Pat Hearn sings, and Stephen Saban, had a photo exhibit at Limelight. One male film critic with an offbeat earring (actually just a dimestore plastic ornament) was approached at Pizza-A-Go-Go by someone curating a jewelry show at Vox Populi. Voila—now he's a bona fide jewelry designer. "I play guitar," one East Village multitalent was bragging at an art opening, "I also paint, write poetry and am a wonderful juggler." He meant, of course, that he brilliantly juggles careers, but when he learns to do it with balls, too, he might really be a talent to reckon with. The more skills the better, because if you get gonged for one of them, you can pull another rabbit out of your hat and beg for one more chance. Defy expectations. Ignore labels. And mix, match and reassemble however you like. But be prepared for that gong.

"I've had people attack me and throw things," says Kelly, who comes off like an ultrasensitive John Barrymore type, but obviously he can take the abuse. "Anything can go on, and that's why people come." Once, an audience member was screaming expletives at Kelly, who responded by taking a large piece of lightning—part of the set—and clobbering the guy. "The audience loved it. They thought it was part of the show," he laughs. "What ever happens, just go with it."

Slamming the audience over the head with the set may not sound like the show biz we all dreamed of as kids, but it's yet another talent downtowners have to add to their repertoires. It beats going to Broadway auditions and finding that there are no parts for people with spiked hair and that you can't afford to join Equity anyway. For those who don't fit into traditional routes, clubs like Pyramid provide a less degrading alternative. In fact, you might become a star there for the very reasons you were laughed out of that summer stock tryout.

"I'm not six-feet tall and I don't have sandy blond hair," says Joey Arias, a singer with the group Strange Party, who also puts together the continuing serial *Mermaids on Heroin*. "I have a different kind of charisma. I'm not going to go on 'real' auditions and get stereotyped as a limp-wristed fag or a hard-core punk. That's what I always get cast as."

Instead, North Carolina-born Arias works tirelessly in clubs doing characters like Andy and Dali in his satirical variety shows with Ann Magnuson, and working on making *Mermaids*—a tongue-in-cheek, life-sized comic strip with mad doctors, luscious villain-

> ● **John Sex reaches absolute nirvana singing "My Face for the World to See," then opens his eyes and realizes he's playing the Pyramid, not Carnegie Hall. His hair remains hard, though.**

esses, ace reporters, and, of course, mermaids—into more than a cult. "A William Morris agent in Beverly Hills wants it to be the new *Rocky Horror Show*. I want to go just . . . beyond. I want to go for the stars." He's ready for his closeup, Mr. DeMille—as long as it doesn't mean playing one of those stereotyped roles, okay guy?

Arias made his New York debut working as a salesman at Fiorucci—chic for a few weeks during the disco heyday—and styling for Antonio. He first came into real notoriety as a backup singer for the late German performer, Klaus Nomi, whose bizarrely brilliant concerts fused opera, electronics, special effects, disco and teak lipstick into an innovative synthesis still to be topped by downtown today.

"When I sang an aria at Max's Kansas City," Nomi said in 1979, "I felt like I'd really accomplished something. I always thought I had to decide from rock or disco or classical—one thing at a time. But at that point, I realized that I could be the bridge to combine all these things."

At around the same time, Club 57 came into prominence with its irreverent sendups of everything from Wendy Wild's *Solid Gold* (with Gloria Gaynmore singing "I Will Expand") to Scott Wittman's *The Trojan Women* (with Laura Kenyon—later in Broadway's *Nine*—playing Andromache as a hilariously overemphatic Lainie Kazan) to the same writer/director's *The Sound of Music* (Holly Woodlawn as Maria, singing, "My Heels Are Alive" and "Cocaine that stays on my nose and false lashes/These are a few of my favorites, Miss Thing"). There are always stretch marks on our scripts," says Wittman's musical partner Marc Shaiman about the liberties they've taken with classic properties.

But don't tell the current crop of

> ● **Dali and Gala are just two of the endless cornucopia of characters performance artists Joey Arias and Ann Magnuson have pulled out of their hats and trotted around club stages for years. Here they perform their hyperdramatic tongue-in-cheek rendition of these two twentieth-century legends at a club called Beulah Land.**

downtown divas about these groundbreaking efforts, it'll detract from their own delusions of superstardom. Some of the people who work the Pyramid stage three or four times a week lose their grip and actually think—like John Sex did at Club 57—that they've reached the pinnacle. Someone like comic Flo Karp—who does what she calls "Flo Shows," which comment on various aspects of American life—is a rare performer who knows the real story. "I've been very depressed this week," she says, "figuring, now what the fuck do I do? The Pyramid is the best place I've performed at, but I don't want to be thirty and working there. I want to go on Letterman's, but then what? I don't want to be mainstream— I don't want to be gross, you know?— but I want to make money. God I don't want to be too famous—that sounds ridiculous. If I ever get that famous, I won't have to worry." That comment was a "Flo Show" in itself.

Karp, whose favorite TV show is "The Love Connection," gently lampoons everything from trendies to shopping to day-glo—often to a crowd of trendies who've just gone shopping for day-glo. "You can find something in everything to parody," she says. "I find things just in everyday life. My humor isn't about easy haha's. It takes some thinking. Some people think it's too esoteric—no, don't say esoteric. That sounds snooty." Boys and girls, can you say esoteric?

Karp has a few things in common with the Alien Comic, who also doesn't tell jokes per se, yet you find yourself laughing before you have time to figure out why you shouldn't be. Maybe it's because he says, "My sister Patsy was such a snob. When she was in her Sunday finery, she wouldn't even look at me," while wearing a demented piece of trash-can chic that's supposed to represent her Sunday finery. Murrin's a double whammy—both funny strange and funny haha. That performance, incidentally, was done right before Easter. His shows always have a theme—not to mention Crazy Glue—holding them together. His philosophy? "I'm not afraid to look ridiculous."

Few downtown performers are. Certainly not Ethyl Eichelberger, the tallest drag queen in New York, even in flats, not to mention a theatrical hairdresser and a classical actor who does twisted variations on the classic female roles like Medea, Lucrezia Borgia, Nefertiti and . . . Auntie Bellum? Ethyl's a classic unto himself. All around the world, drag performers lip-sync to Shirley Bassey's "This Is My Life," but Ethyl would probably do Shirley Bassey as Lola Montez. Downtown drag involves more than moving your lips and flailing your arms, it's a much more subversive means for the unexpected.

"It's not enough to put on a dress and go on stage and that's the end of it," says John Kelly. "That's the beginning of it." So Ethyl, a sometimes associate of Ridiculous Theatrical Company legend Charles Ludlam, makes himself up garishly, turns an accordion into an accessory, and transforms *Hamlet* into *Hamlette*, with such non-Shakespearean exchanges as:

"The cream always rises to the top."
"Well, so does scum."

"Did Hamlet have sex with Ophelia?"
"In the Chicago Company he did, in Cincinnati it was with Horatio."

Dozens of costume changes and a healthy dose of slapstick help make this travesty—um, tragedy—a *Hamlette* with the emphasis on the ham.

Also in the cast are Miss Hapi Phace (Mark Phredd) and Tabboo! (Stephen Tashjian), who undoubtedly rank among the more spontaneous creations of Alphabetland. Phredd, who's made a career out of ugliness, looks like Herman Munster trying to be Madonna and not even vaguely succeeding. For years, friends encouraged him to go into show biz—there's apparently a big demand for Herman Munster/Madonna lookalikes—so, he gave up his career as a macrobiotic chef and started at the top—the bartop, that is, dancing go-go at the Pyramid. "I knew I couldn't pass as a woman," he says, perceptively, "so, I pushed the ugly aspect. I wanted to be the ugliest girl of all. People have stared at me and laughed at me on the street for years. I figured now I'd make them pay to do it."

With the most infectious good spirits he'd do that—the most terrifying smile since Carol Channing—and make them feel all the more guilty for ever having ridiculed him. This was the most ambitious vendetta since Bette Davis's daughter wrote her memoirs, but it was a vendetta of niceness. "Some people can't stand how optimistic I can be," he says. "I've always had a Hapi Phace thing to the point where it drives people crazy. But I figured, since a lot of the downtown ecosystem is based on nihilism, it would be a different thing to be positive and good. It was an experiment, and the reaction was great the first time. People wanted Hapi Phace. They didn't want to wear black and be morbid, they wanted to wear colors and have fun." What Phredd didn't realize was that he'd now have to eat Hapi, sleep Hapi and wake up screaming Hapi. He'd be expected to be a windup Sandy Duncan doll running through fields of Wheat Thins and giggling all the time. *Help!* "If I don't walk around smiling, people scream at me. And I realize that it's basically Hapi that gets invited to the parties and pays my rent and takes me out to dinner." Trapped by his own creation. Still, it's a whole lot better than being a macrobiotic chef anyday.

Tashjian—aka Tabboo!—is also a victim, in a sense, of his own competence. He's become a Pyramid celebrity with all its glories and all its limitations, too. "Downtown celebrity only gets you so far," he says. "I want to be Ann-Margret." That part's already taken, unfortunately. But in go-go boots, a vinyl mini and a mohair sweater, Tabboo! cuts a striking figure of her own. She's a kooky blithe spirit—a monster who thinks she's a goddess—and that's only one side of Tashjian who's also written a rap song about Armenians through the ages (Cher, Mike Connors and Adrienne Barbeau, among others); mastered a variety of instruments, including the trombone ("I'm the new vaudeville sensation"); helped pick Pat Hearn's dress at her wedding ("Her conservative sister told me to take off the mink tails"); and is "a naive primitive" artist with several gallery shows to his credit. His forte? Portraits of drag queens.

Once a puppeteer in Worcester, Massachusetts, he remembers putting on shows of drag puppets fighting bitchily. "The kids would throw shoes at me, and I'd take the money and run." In the late 1970s, he was a collage artist, "but that doesn't get you very far." And though he still paints, he says, "Painting is the private, alcoholic lifestyle. It's lonely, and that's why I discovered *The Power for Living*—my personal relationship with Elizabeth Taylor."

The twenty-six-year-old claims he's been doing drag for twenty-six years, and adds, "Tabboo! is something deep within me yearning to come out." What it is exactly no one's figured out yet, but it probably has something to do with the thrill of performing and the need for acceptance. If anyone at the Pyramid throws shoes at him now, it's only because they're fabulous and they think they would look good on him. "They love me at the Pyramid," he says, as if hearing canned applause no one else can hear, "but I've been a serious actress and now I want Vegas." He has the primary qualification—he's never repeated an outfit.

Tashjian's determined to take his go-go earrings to the glittering heights, even if he has to be sincere to get there. "MGM making you over at five-thirty a.m. doesn't happen anymore," he says, as if this is headline news. "You have to be independent today. You have to be Robert De Niro." He pauses, thoughtfully. "I wouldn't mind that." Well Robert De Niro would probably mind, and Tashjian would be better off sticking to that Ann-Margret dream anyway.

At the Pyramid, the Now Explosion—a group of porn connoisseurs, art school dropouts, hot bachelors and paparazzi from Atlanta—emerge through "the world's largest vagina" (as they proudly bill it) and sing aggressively raunchy but lovable songs like "Hot Snatch" and "Mandingo." Their special guest star is Lady Bunny, the queen mother of drag queens, moonlighting from the sci-fi/R&B group Shazork, who is frenetically go-go dancing herself into a veritable now explosion. In the audience are the cast of *Mama Said*, wearing buttons that promote their play—a saga of tormented Times Square hairdressers. They carry on with all the self-congratulation of recent Oscar winners, and you feel like a heretic for not treating them as such. "Victims of pretense" coos a drag queen diva who reeks uncomfortably of rubbing alcohol. (Did she make a mistake and dab herself with the cheap swill she puts in expensive designer bottles so house guests will think it's eau-de-God-knows-what?)

Christina, a dominatrix with a pronounced (and pronouncedly bogus) German accent, is there, emitting a flow of psychobabble that's as mesmerizing as it is disturbing. "I just had a baby, and I'm already sick to death of the damned thing," she says, flinging her little darling—actually a cheap blond wig—to the floor and cackling with self-satisfaction. Sylvia Miles is there too, in an outfit of inspired cacophony, saying how strangers yell "Madonna" when they see her, but that she's also gotten comments relating her to Cyndi Lauper and Tina Turner. Even at the Pyramid though she'd prefer to be known as Sylvia Miles, actress. Video artist Nelson Sullivan is there, too, documenting everyone's fabulousness along with their most embarrassing Foulups, Bloopers, Blunders and Faux Pas, hoping people will either want to procure a copy from him for posterity or maybe pay him to burn the master tape. "The scene makes me feel young again," he says, pausing only because his batteries have gone dead. "It's so fully created and finished, all I usually need to do is come in, focus and take its picture."

The next night he's shooting Atlanta's androgynous sensation, RuPaul Charles, who's doing a takeoff on Diana Ross—possibly without even knowing it—singing his theme song, "Sex Freak," and telling the grungy audience, "In my heart I love you—you know that." But downstairs, on the video screen, the feature attraction isn't RuPaul doing "Reach Out and Touch," it's the diaphanous diva starring in *Trilogy of Terror*, in which he's mercilessly violated by a crowbar, at which point a friend walks in and exclaims, "Sheila! You didn't tell me you were having a party!" RuPaul is the only black white trash in the world.

Stay tuned and the video here might also include the work of Tom Rubnitz, a Chicago-born video artist whose inspirations run all the way from *That Girl* to Lee Harvey Oswald—"the first media blitz of my life"—and who somehow fuses all those conflicting influences into a consistent style. Rubnitz's *Made for TV*, a fifteen-minute film seen on PBS, has Ann Magnuson portraying a staggering variety of TV characters, changing persons with each flick of the imaginary dial. From a morning show host promising to tell about "How to deal with a death in the family . . . the growing number of holiday highway fatalities . . . and how to pack for a weekend" to a hyperactive MTV v.j. to an insipid coffee drinker ("Mmm . . . this is mountain grown") to a hyperactive MTV star (Linda Hagendazovich), Magnuson is always right on target right up to the quick-cutting madness that leads to the TV burnout at the end. But Rubnitz will never be burned out on TV, he is obsessed. Another of his clips has Bobby Bradley in a touching testimonial: "I used to have neurasthenia. Now, I'm cured. I'm a famous bowling star."

Rubnitz's work takes off on all the clichés of pop culture and domesticity, but his bite is remarkably benign. "It's a celebration of life," he says. "I've been described as being in a *PM Magazine* vein, which I like a lot. It's closer to real life than art. It's a slice of life served up with humor. I find life very funny and tragic."

And that's an apt description for life at the Pyramid, "Probably cliquish," he says, "but those are my friends. Besides, people can enter into it. I've met so many new people there recently—they just keep on coming. There are some really amazing kids. For a while, I got discouraged about the statistics of kids who are Reaganites and want something safe like a marriage and a job. I felt the world was doomed. But after meeting some of the new crowd, I don't feel that way anymore. I'm optimistic about life in general. But then again, I haven't been to England in two years."

A trip to La Mama, at this point, would probably be more inspirational. There, a brilliant up-and-coming comic named Danitra Vance—whose humor is more pointed and less saccharine than Whoopi Goldberg's (But who's comparing?)—gives Magnuson's split personalities a run for their schizophrenia. She satirizes everything—from bogus faith healers ("I'm a pyromaniac and I'm here to light up your life") to strippers ("Call me ma'am in honor of my mammary glands") to performance artists ("We are all spinach and brussels sprouts on crutches!")—with mercurial mood changes and boundless energy. How can a talent this immense remain underground? Just as you wonder this, you learn that the person taking notes next to you is a recruiter for "Star Search." Vance is going to make it big, even if it means going on that show. Shortly after that you learn that *Saturday Night Live* has conducted their own search and made her a regular. Whoopi!

At Danceteria, Joey Arias and Ann Magnuson are debuting two new shows: *Family*, the tribal love rock musical, in which they play not the Brady bunch, but Charles Manson and Squeaky Fromme (backed by the Spahn Ranch Hand Dancers); and *Murray and Gloria!*, in which they're the even more horrifying Murray Schwartzbergsteinfeld and Gloria Fowler, two whiny West Coast obnoxos who read *Variety* through Foster Grants, pick their teeth and have constant think-tank meetings. If they did this show in LA, the audience would probably find the characters endearing, but then the same would probably be the case with the Manson musical.

The Danceteria audience? They react as enthusiastically as they would to anything that tears away at the American mainstream with any wit. Just the tearing-down act isn't enough anymore. Now, there must be method to the madness. Even drugs are done more with a sense of purpose; you're more likely to get high for a specific event than as a way of life. And that event had better be more than just someone throwing up on stage. Tastelessness must be topical, and anger must be distilled into clever lines. You can hold Johnny Lydon up as a role model until you drop, but it's the rebels who can temper their outrage with a heavy coating of accessiblity who make it beyond the club scene. Cyndi Lauper is the sweetest punk moll you could take home to meet mother and Billy Idol is so obviously affecting that sneer, he'd probably (like Norman Bates in *Psycho*) have trouble hurting a fly. But who remembers *Psycho* after seeing *Pshyco III—The Musical*?

The nicest of the downtown anti-heros, and the least likely to throw up on stage (it's not aesthetically appealing; besides, he'd want to turn it into a production number) is Charles Busch, a drag performer whose shows at the Limbo Lounge brought him the kind of adoring audience that only stopped laughing so they could hear the next line. There was cause for their devotion; Busch's extreme likability, even—or especially—when he's being vicious, his economy of words and movement, and his total extravagance of wigs and costumes made him both the king and queen of undiscovered New York theater. Busch, like Eichelberger, plays the great diva roles—in his case, *Theodora—She-Bitch of Byzantium*, 1940s nightclub chanteuse Irish O'Flannagan (in *Times Square Angel*), stage actress Madeleine Astarte (in *Vampire Lesbians of Sodom*) and Gidget. Like John Kelly, his act only begins the second he's in drag. "The dress gives me a lot more confidence," he says. "I couldn't even raise my hand in class, but when I have the dress and makeup on, I'm not myself. I'm this actress."

And like Tashjian, he has special affection for Ann-Margret, so much so that in *Vampire Lesbians*, when the time frame suddenly jumps from Sodom to modern day Las Vegas, he appears in an Ann-Margret wig bunched off to one side and sings "Maniac," backed by four frantic male dancers in fringed midriff T-shirts. When Busch reaches the line about how "I'm dancing like I've never danced before," the chorines hoof themselves into a frenzy while he, à la Lauren Bacall, merely stands immobile and slightly alters his arm gestures. The crowd goes wild.

The Busch troupe, directed impeccably by Kenneth Elliott, found a home at the Limbo, a performance space near Avenue C started by Michael Gormley (aka Michael Limbo) in a former garage. "I'd never been east of First Avenue a few years ago," says Busch. "We went to the old Limbo Lounge one night and it was so tacky, like a railroad stop. There was no stage at all and only a couple of clamp-on lights. The audience was walking through the stage during the show. Somehow, I thought it would be fun to do a show there for our own amusement." It turned out to be for a lot of people's amusement; the troupe's irreverent high camp brought a gay crowd who normally wouldn't go anywhere Donna Summer records weren't being played, all the way East for the first time. "And sometimes we did get some straight people," he laughs.

When the Limbo moved to a bigger space, the troupe took the upward leap with it, but we're still not exactly talking the Winter Garden. "The dressing room was the size of a coffee table," says Busch, exaggerating (it was actually smaller than a coffee table). But it beat playing Indiana, which Busch did and lived to tell about it. ("It was like *It's a Wonderful Life*. I saw all these guys who were like me ten years earlier. The place had stagnated in 1972—a lot of hot pants and chains and blow-dried hair.")

As a result of their Limbo triumphs, the troupe moved to a very respectable off-Broadway theater, the Provincetown Playhouse, where they received rave reviews and played for a whole new audience who didn't have to crawl through rubble to discover Busch's glittering talents. The amazing media approval of Busch, even from the straightest of old fogies, made him into an acceptable adventure for everyone, many of whom found themselves snickering into their three-piece-suit collars for the first twenty minutes before letting go with shameless out-and-out hysteria that said they were happy to be part of Busch's breakthrough. The word spread, and soon the diva was negotiating a movie deal (West Coast Productions of the *Vampire Lesbians/Sleeping Beauty* double bill), and no doubt bigger dressing rooms. Busch might even get to Broadway some day (maybe Tuesday). But somehow no matter what happens, his Limbo Lounge days will go down in theater legend as his truly glamorous ones.

The doyenne of drag artists, Charles Ludlam, certainly feels more attachment to his own self-contained off-Broadway theater company than to the other, "bigger" credits on his resume. In fact, not only doesn't Ludlam mind being New York's best-kept secret, he loves it. The Ridiculous Theatrical Company founder/star has purposely kept his above-ground exposure to a rarefied minimum. He did a "Today" show that aired at seven in the morning on New Year's Day, when even if anyone saw it, they were definitely too drunk to remember. He did a "Candid Camera" episode years ago, sitting in a bathtub for eight hours to confuse secretaries. And he wore $20,000 worth of fox furs for his appearance as a romance writer on "Oh, Madeline," the short-lived TV sitcom starring his old Hofstra University buddy, Madeline Kahn.

• Charles Busch slayed 'em as *Theodora—She-Bitch of Byzantium* at Gracie Mansion's sculpture garden before the grand diva brought his irreverent and sparklingly funny mayhem to larger spaces.

Your average person has probably never even heard of Ludlam, though they'd rightly assume he has something to do with bedlam. The actor/writer/director says there are even longtime New Yorkers who insist they wouldn't dream of going all the way down to the Village to see his plays. These are people for whom Lincoln Center is downtown.

Yet, even if the blue-creme-rinsed ladies never see him, there are tremendous advantages to Ludlam's specialized seclusion. He has total freedom and near-total adulation. He doesn't have to worry about moving to Broadway and having both the opening and closing party on the same night. "I chose the high-art route," he says, sounding like the grand diva he is. "You can always take a week off from high art and do something else, but you can't take a week off from something else and do high art." Ludlam adds that he's able to "keep the bullshit to a minimum" and make things "very human and very amusing." He's done so well in the off-Broadway setting that he could fringe his dresses with all the Obie Awards he's won. But they'd make better earrings.

Sure, he'd like to bring his work to a larger audience, but he'd rather not deal with the compromising situations that kind of "success" sometimes puts an artist in. "The people who put money into my plays are giving me a contribution. They never want to see it again. But Broadway investors want money in return. So, it is a whole different kind of money. And then, of course, so many people have to like it. Not that many people have to like my plays, which is nice.

"On Broadway," he continues, "you can potentially make much more money, but astronomical amounts can be lost, too. And if you indulge in a very long run, it means being stuck in that one play." At the Ridiculous Theatrical Company, Ludlam doesn't have to feel "stuck" in anything. He could read the phone book if he felt like it, and his audience would still think it's better than *Cats*.

He has no actual ties to the downtown scene, except that he does his plays on Sheridan Square and makes his own rules. He never telegraphs his humor, preferring to get unexpected laughs that often come out of serious situations, and he never alters things just to please the audience, which actually pleases them just fine. So, in that respect, Ludlam has a very downtown spirit. He doesn't pander to expectations, thriving instead on carrying out his own creative instincts. "I do what I want, and I'm usually right," he says, laughing but meaning it. Uptown, Ludlam might get stared at. Downtown, if he's stared at, it's purely the ogle of respect.

9

The Not So Defiant Ones »

The Fabulous Pop Tarts—Randy Pop and Fenton Tart—sing about the "New York City Beat" at Danceteria's fourth floor, Congo Bill, with verve.

Dropping the right performing arts' boldfaces is as crucial to survival on the party circuit as procuring drink tickets. It's important to know who's hot, and nowadays the most established, obvious names are just as valid as the most esoteric. Liberace can be mentioned in the same sentence as Meredith Monk without any loss of credibility and Peewee Herman can be debated as fervently as Butch Morris, whoever that is. (He's the cornet player and leader of an improvisational "new music" ensemble, okay?)

The days when downtown exclusively delighted in spitting in the face of mass culture are now just a thread in David Bowie's zoot suit. As the avant-garde started running out of ideas and verging on self-parody, downtown's attention span got a little shorter and more rooted in the real world, (i.e. *New York Post* headlines). All the same people who've ever wanted to push a mime face-front right into the Central Park mud would feel the same urge when confronted with an ultraserious performance piece about a roach motel, for example.

Sure downtown still likes Philip Glass, but he's the most accessible of "avant-garde" composers, lending his talent to everything from dance rock groups to Hollywood films. They like Laurie Anderson, too, the ultimate performance artist who even approached her early career as a teacher of art history as a performance. ("That was really when I first began doing performance because basically I was not an art historian and I just forgot a lot of the facts, so I'd just make them up.") But Anderson's art takes off on identifiable emblems of mass culture, from phone machines to plane rides to shopping malls and often manages to have an idiosyncratic danceable electronic beat. She intones her bizarre little vignettes with all the warmth and willingness of a kindergarten teacher. "To me," she told *New Musical Express*, "things have just gotten a little airier. And by that I mean we're now more dependent on things which come through the air—radio and TV and those signals that are becoming almost as real as the three-dimensional world is to people. And this is very very strange." It's that very two-dimensional airiness that Anderson frequently comments on, thereby making herself more accessible to her audience, who loves the fact that a prestige act like hers doesn't have to be boring. As one critic said of her, she has all the trappings of art, yet she's "easy," and given a chance, people will always opt for art that's easy.

Talking Heads are constantly breaking new musical ground, but largely in connection with the use of familiar elements like reggae, sixties soul music and even country-western. Their 1985 album, "Little Creatures," was aptly described by one writer as a record you could play for your parents. Both the Heads and Anderson have been hailed a bit too insistently by the *New York Times* and, as a result, embraced too eagerly by the middle class, who find them the most adorable of wild, experimental artists. That fills downtowners with dread—What good's a wild, experimental artist who's a household name? It also arouses the sneaking suspicion that these people might be creative crackpots as surely as they are genuine geniuses, but the media can only dilute their efficacy to a degree. As long as these performers remain in touch, they'll remain in favor.

The thread of identifiability, of spoofing and yet extolling popular culture, is the key to downtown's applause meter right now. Charles Ludlam's impersonation of a Maria Callas-type opera diva named Galas, who keeps files on who's seen her various outfits and lives with the knowledge that she only has eighty-six *Norma*s left in her throat, was greeted as not only funny, but delicious gossip-as-theater. *Pagliacci* done at La Mama with untrained singers not adhering to the usual vocal ranges, offered a fresh hearing of a classic, and hey, it was still classic. Ping Chong's multimedia *Nosferatu* breathes similar life into another oldie but goodie, giving it the luster of the new along with the lingering comfort of familiarity. This performance piece combined a Kabuki-style prologue, projections and an architectural environment into a short work that provoked a variety of reactions, boredom not usually among them.

Musical revues such as *Downtown Divas* and *Downtown Dukes* demonstrate just how much this video-age crowd likes its entertainment quick and full of familiar references. These shows, produced by Gabriel Rotello at Limelight, feature a succession of up-and-coming singers doing short and entertaining turns that show them off to their most glittering advantage. The *Divas* and *Dukes* shows are a microcosm of everything that is and isn't happening on the scene.

Occasionally, there's a throwback to a more jagged punk style—like "Downtown Duke" Ned Sublette's aggressive and strangely arresting yelp—but on his song, "I Ain't Afraid of Girls," the band stopped and started so many times, cmcee Holly Woodlawn mistakenly introduced the next singer in the middle of it. Unfortunately, there's little patience for that kind of idiosyncracy anymore. Mostly, the emphasis is on camp, nostalgia and show biz, with punk aggressiveness distilled into witty and danceable music.

The best example of that is "Duke" Dean Johnson, who does funny, opinionated raps, which are bursting with an anger that's made more agreeable by the fact that the expletives are worked into clever rhymes. Johnson is six-feet-six, gangly, bald and compelling on stage. "I can't remember your name and I could not care less," he raps in one song called "Fuck You." "I could have more fun talking to the IRS/Why don't you take your problems to analysis?/Take your foot out of your mouth and suck on this/Fuck you!" The audience, rather than being offended, chants the title along with him. Those in the know react even more loudly when Johnson does his Teri Toye rap: "There's not a woman who is scarier, Teri/But can you get me into Area, Teri?" If America ever gets over its fear of 6'6" bald men in dresses screaming "Fuck you!" this guy could go places.

Fifteen-year-old Emanon Johnson (no relation) an Apollo Theater favorite, performs "Baby Beat Box"—an amazing *a cappella* symphony of sound in which he creates an entire hip-hop orchestra by dexterously maneuvering his tireless mouth (easy for him to say). The Fabulous Pop Tarts, a perky British duo, syncopate on "New York City Beat," their danceable, up-tempo mix of disco, rap and street smarts. Zette does a guest appearance, singing his own composition that goes, "You'll never be the man your mother was/You'll never be the girl your father was" and renders it so hypnotically it almost makes sense. And Hoy Boy flaunts his early rock and roll roots by swinging to "Let the Good Times Roll."

Buxom "diva" Kristi Rose, who fanatics feel is Patsy Cline reincarnate, packs a wallop belting out the country standard "Only Make Believe," and the equally formidable Lina Koutrakos delivers Gene Pitney's "Town Without Pity" without anyone needing to tell her to "Sing out, Louise!" Earl Scooter does some stinging blues/rock in "Man's World" and Debbie Cole, who sang on Malcolm McLaren's "Madame Butterfly," delivers a dynamic "Rescue Me" by Fontella Bass. The crowd cheers—these people are more interested in classic pop songs right now than they are in potentially offputting artistic statements.

There's still a proliferation of exotic and innovative sounds, but because of the lessened demand for them by the cool crowd, the showcases for new music have lost the glow of chic. CBGB and Irving Plaza still offer tough and energetic local bands like the Vipers and Pedantiks and the Reggae Lounge serves up a steady flow of the hypnotic "Rasta" beat to satisfy the increasing swell of interest in reggae. Two of the most progressive clubs—SOB's (Sounds of Brazil) and the Lone Star—started as a Brazilian and a country bar, respectively, then diversified to feature a staggering variety of musical acts from seminal new waver Arto Lindsay, Senegalese jazz group (via France) Toure Kunda, the former leader of Black Uhuru Michael Rose and the queen of salsa Celia Cruz at SOB's to zydeco, rockabilly, James Brown and Chubby Checker at Lone Star.

But even though the aural anarchy of bands like the Butthole Surfers still finds an audience, more likely the fashion crowd is drawn to the satirical, heavy-on-the-horn-section dance rock of groups like Strange Party (even though their "Imitators" bursts the bubble of fashion trend-followers) and the Lounge Lizards, whose anarchy is couched in familiar components of American music. Interest in American pop history runs so strongly that rock star David Johansen found a whole second-career wind as his alter ego, Buster

Pointdexter, a bespectacled singer of rousing, sing-along-or-else party numbers like "Gimme a Pigfoot" and "If You're So Smart, How Come You Ain't Rich?" These are songs that he always wanted to sing, and it turns out everyone always wanted to hear them.

A group called Street the Beat had a run of many months in the basement of Pizza-A-Go-Go doing covers of Beatles songs with such attention to detail people could close their eyes and fantasize that it was a Fab Four reunion. Crowds love it when the Fabulous Pop Tarts rest their "New York City Beat" for a minute and do their fairly straightforward electronic version of Irene Cara's hit, "Fame." Television merits the most appreciation, though, probably because it's free and disposable fun. *Details* General Manager Ricky Spears has weekly "Dynasty" dinners in honor of that awfulest of wonderful shows. These events treat each weekly installment as if it were exalted drama not only to eat by but to live by. Spears sometimes encourages the guests to dress like the characters from the show and sometimes the real-life drama that ensues surpasses that on the TV screen. The menu? Anything from roast baby squab, made to celebrate Krystle's baby (whipped up "with a pinch of irony and a dash of bad taste") to ruthless salad with vengeful dressing in honor of Blake, who might become even more ruthless and vengeful if he heard about these dinners. But downtown loves them.

It's all a symptom of the fact that the scene's not insulated anymore, feeding off the outside world as voraciously as the reverse phenomenon occurs, though downtown usually feeds off for entertainment value while the outside world does it for money. Downtowners are wide open for communication—phones are a virtual extension of their bodies—and ready for influences as long as they're either very classic or very new. (Coca Cola is the perfect downtown product for that very reason.)

The interest, though, is sometimes carried out a little grudgingly. Publicly, a lot of New York style-setters have nothing but disdain for London trends, but as soon as there's a free minute, all the same people pack up their disdain and run over to British fashion liaison Susanne Bartsch's SoHo store, which showcases the newest and best of the London designers. Running into someone in this miracle of obelisks, deco pagodas, mirrors and tile is akin to running into someone in a porno shop. Keep your eyes down and mutter something to the effect that you're just meeting friends there, not that they're really close friends. Really close friends wouldn't be interested in British fashion, ah-hem.

Even when London's Body Map crew of fashion-victim jewelry designers, makeup artists and self-promoters—"The Disco Modeling School," as they call themselves—hit our shores with a vengeance, downtown observed from a disturbed distance. These people could make the old Sprouse-Toye-Meisel clique look like the Von Trapp family, but they're much friendlier. They're even friendlier if there's a camera within a mile, an envelope worth going to the opening of or a large speaker on which they can go-go dance until the last drop of attention is wrenched from the guest of honor. They are appallingly fabulous to the bone, and downtown jealousy pretends not to like them.

The sneer fades quickly enough. The downtown experience depends on accepting new arrivals (read: rivals) like these, however distasteful that may be. It's crucial to be open to the unexpected—to that pinch of bad taste—because the scene hits you with a barrage of tasteless absurdities that don't let up and you'd better be ready for them. Events and people continually strive to shock, but what's shocking to Joe Normal would barely make a seasoned scenemaker flinch. To the jaded, who've been hit with the barrage before, they're just amusing entertainment.

Clubs feature male strip shows, "Best Butt" competitions and porn star Leo Ford gleefully masturbating on stage after his opening act—a group called Killer Pussy—gets the crowd appropriately moist. Some of these events are not legal, so clubs bill them as private parties, warning that there's no admittance without an invitation.

For the now defunct electronic group Soft Cell, Danceteria hosted a perfectly legal, if wantonly outrageous "Nonstop Erotic Cabaret" full of sex-related spectacles. "We rented twenties porn films and intercut them with religious images," says Merrill Aldighieri, who curated the video for the evening, along with her husband, Joe Tripician. She adds, "We used Jackie Kennedy's tour of the White House for a voiceover."

Aldighieri and Tripician, who run an alternative video company called Co-Directions, met when they both answered an ad for video animation apprentices for "The Muppet Show." ("When I saw the ad," says Merrill, "I knew I'd meet someone foxy.") They both got jobs, doing screen tests for potential new Muppets—a step up from Merrill's former job "doing Fellini-style interviews with dogcatchers" for a California cable program. Eventually, they found their true metier in club video, helping pioneer the medium at Hurrah, where Merrill fondly remembers the Fleshtones' lead singer, Peter Zaremba, "sat on my head" while she tried to film the group in performance. Eventually, Zaremba, wacky guy, pulled the camera out of her hand and started shooting the video himself. When in doubt, shoot your own videos.

The "Nonstop Erotic Cabaret" night was a success, but the husband-and-wife team ran into trouble on another night when a club manager objected to their showing Little Black Sambo cartoons, insisting it was a racist choice. The same manager once told video artist Maureen Nappi that showing the Plasmatics' videos "wasn't exactly feminist." "I'd say, 'It's very feminist. I want to see her breasts. It's liberating'," remembers Nappi.

She won out. Restrictions like that rarely come to much on this scene, except to fuel artist's drives to do more verboten and offensive things. When the Avenue B gallery, playing host to an irreverent and very graphic show called "Feminist and Misogynist Together at Last," got an outraged letter saying, "Can it be that anyone thinks that feminism is funny or that it's a personality disorder?", they hardly took down the exhibit in shame. In fact they proudly posted the letter on the wall, making it a part of the show.

All the downtown artists love seizing the chance to slap the uptight in the face, as composer Wendy Chambers eloquently bears out in the nicest way possible. Just as graffiti brought art into the streets, Chambers has helped turn music into mammoth public events. It was she who had twenty-four musician friends of hers floating in rowboats on Central Park Lake and playing her cacophonous strains while a sea of aghast spectators applauded wildly, even when the tuba player capsized. It was Chambers who had twelve people at the Kitchen (appropriately named, for once) playing cookie sheets and cake pans with spatulas while a blender chorus played "puree," "mix" and other nutritional selections. She also had nine drivers beeping their horns to waltz tunes while aligning their cars in various formations and an artist painting on a canvas hooked up to contact mikes so that every dab of the brush became loud, avant-garde music. ("I conceived a painting as music itself," says the hyperenthusiastic Chambers, who wasn't even upset when a glob of paint went accidentally hurling towards the wall. It created a sort of music of its own.) And anyone who was within a half-mile of Washington Square Park one September afternoon in 1979 no doubt remembers hearing hundreds of people with portable radios simultaneously tuned into the "Close Encounters Theme" on WBAI while a band played along.

What makes this bellbottomed girl from Westfield, New Jersey, a candidate for rapt attention rather than the men in white suits? That she's stretched the stodgy realm of classical music into the environs and activities of everyday life—driving, carousing in the park, cooking and listening to the radio. She's made mass entertainment out of the sheer spectacle of creating music.

"I don't want to do a musical piece just for the piece alone," she says. "I have to have a purpose for doing something, even if it's just shaking people up. Christo was an inspiration for me. I was totally amazed that he went out and spent three million dollars to build that twenty-four-mile-long fence. I figured anything I might want to do is a lot simpler."

But what's the point Wendy? Or is there one, huh? "I guess it's just the challenge of getting all those people together, uplifting their spirits. Just to show that you can do whatever you think of if you put your mind to it."

Madonna may well be the queen of two downtown cultural phenomena—outrageousness and feeding off. The singer, who told *Newsweek* that she "latched onto him [her junior high school ballet teacher] like a leech and took everything I could from him," also told them, "I'm very career oriented. You are attracted to men who have material things because that's what pays the rent and buys you furs. That's the security. That lasts longer than emotion." This is the same person who wears a crucifix as she spins around, thrusting her navel intriguingly at the camera.

Madonna's not unlike the leading character, played by Susan Berman, in Susan Seidelman's *Smithereens*, who says, "I'm really rotten" as she tries to wangle her way up the stairway to rock and roll heaven-on-earth. The singer unceremoniously dumped Mark Kamins, her original producer, and has gone through ups and downs with her ex-boyfriend and sometime-producer John "Jellybean" Benitez, though amazingly neither one of them has a bad word to say about the disco babydoll. Kamins says it's only natural that someone as successful as Madonna should get bad press, besides, he laughs, "I had royalties on the album, so I'm not complaining." Jellybean, who recently worked with the singer again on the film *Street Smart* says simply, "We've always been friends. We always will be friends."

Madonna's calculated moves towards fame—"Clawing her way to stardom half-naked," as *Newsweek* put it—have been an inspiration to downtown achievers. Still, the slogan artist Barbara Kruger came up with for the last Whitney Biennial does come to mind: "When I hear the word culture, I take out my checkbook." Fortunately, Madonna's music is contagiously danceable and she almost redeemed all past transgressions with her role as Susan, the blithe-spirited drifter who was desperately being sought in Susan Seidelman's *Desperately Seeking Susan*. Madonna's Susan was totally self-absorbed in adorable ways that made her an unself-consciously endearing cross between Marilyn Monroe and Judy Holliday. You couldn't help loving her for being so aimless. You couldn't help admiring her for being kind of a user. She meant well, after all.

And Madonna did well. It didn't hurt the film's success that the singer—who, when the film started, was a mere up-and-comer whom Orion was understandably underwhelmed about—had become so popular by the time the film came out that people were buying imitation Madonna moles. But it was especially serendipitous that she was so damned good.

NYU Grad Film School alumna Seidelman's first film, the independent feature *Smithereens* (1982), was pulled together for a mere $80,000, a modern-day cinema miracle befitting someone who would later work with a Madonna. It paid off handsomely for all involved, especially Seidelman.

The movie is the story of an East Village (via New Jersey) groupie's quest for fame despite a pervasive lack of talent, and it did well enough to catch the attention of the major companies. That led to *Susan*, a much bigger-budgeted but still very economical movie that hit with critics and audiences alike. Rosanna Arquette and Madonna played two opposites who switched roles as a result of that hoariest of Hollywood cliches, amnesia. Despite that plot twist, *Susan* was a giddy screwball excursion that benefited a lot from the presence of downtown regulars and locations and from the hip sensibility Seidelman had obviously honed in her previous film immersion into the Lower East Side. It was also an inspiration to all independent filmmakers who suddenly thought, "I could have a hit movie someday too."

Seidelman, like her heroines, grew up in the suburbs and told the *Village Voice*, "It was your basic 1960s split-level development outside Philadelphia, with a shopping mall and a Dunkin' Donuts." In *Susan*, she and screenwriter Leora Barish managed to contrast that very way of life with the ultracool downtown world and come up with a balance that even people who weren't twelve-year-old "Wannabe" girls could appreciate. This wasn't a slice of pure, unbridled downtown served up without aesthetic seasoning. It was the scene's sensibility given a glossy Hollywood coating and a suburban point of reference. While taking Seidelman to the next logical career step, it preserved her style and thought processes. And it was mass-palatable.

Many future Seidelmans have already struggled and created for years, desperately seeking money to scrape films together and places to show them. Around the time of clubs like Mudd, Club 57, and Tier 3 a place called the New Cinema, set in a storefront space on St. Marks Place, showcased the work of low-budget filmmakers who couldn't exactly show up at the Ziegfeld Theatre with a print of their latest thousand-dollar oeuvre. Becky Johnston set it up along with fellow filmmakers James Nares and Eric Mitchell, "so films could have a pretty extended run and get some kind of prolonged attention." Unfortunately, nine months after the New Cinema opened, Johnston and friends were evicted because they weren't paying rent for the summer months during which they weren't open.

"I think it was a big success, though," says Nares, the offbeat creator of the ninety-minute, $3,000-epic *Rome '78* (a deliciously decadent version of the ancient Rome story starring David McDermott, Lance Loud and other staples of the scene at the time). *Rome '78*, which had a healthy run at the New Cinema, was easily the best film to come out of that wave. The cheapo toga comedy was so earnest in putting its cast of punks and slatterns into a Roman milieu (it was filmed largely at Columbia University) and so amateurish in execution that it's practically irresistible. The discombobulated plot, containing a litany of every ancient sin and debauchery, outdoes even *Caligula*, with which it should be paired on a double bill in a smoky Times Square theater. Most weeks of the year, though, *Rome '78* just sits in a box in James Nares' apartment.

Scott and Beth B's *The Offenders*, a fifties-style melodrama that was serialized at Max's Kansas City in eight weekly segments, is another seminal film of the era, *The Maltese Falcon* for people who'd been Bowery Bogarts for years without even knowing it. It's compelling filmmaking, a little rough around the edges, but mostly as fresh as that day's headlines, starring such Lower East Side luminaries as John Lurie and ex-Contortion Adele Bertei and filled with cartoonlike violence that spices up an already pretty arresting plot. When asked if they mind people calling the film violent and sexist, both Billingsleys (their full name) dryly said, "I hope they'll call it something."

Even now, whether these films are set in ancient Rome or on White Street, similar themes and styles link them. Many rework Hollywood clichés—detective stories are popular, often centering on misfits looking in from the outside. Many redefine formal conventions—sometime-club-doorman George Haas's "Romance", about a gay airline steward who finds solace in an obese woman who's a fallen radical from the sixties, is only fifty minutes long. According to the production notes, "The length is the result of the letting go of the description 'feature film' (minimum seventy-five minutes), deciding instead to make the best film possible." Many, like the four independent shorts shown at the Squat Theatre on a night of "Neo-Narrative Pyrotechnics," create an alienated yet strangely familiar world of Kafkaesque sitcom, the ordinary taken to extraordinary levels of asburdism, much as Laurie Anderson does with her music/performance art.

A lot of the underground filmmakers are struggling. So, they make their characters go through a similar self-denial. They're far more concerned with making a personal statement about alienation than achieving any kind of technical proficiency. If they were given $30 million to do a film, Scott and Beth B once said they'd do ten films. Too many of the Hollywood films, according to another filmmaker, "are mock-Hitlerian, Wagnerian Nazi films with universal scenes like the galaxies colliding as the master races fight it out." Downtown can relate better to more identifiable scenes like trendies colliding at an art opening or maybe pierogis colliding on a combination platter." Don't get them wrong, though. Like the performance artists, as much as these filmmakers practice the poverty aesthetic, it's more out of necessity than desire. A lot of them would turn cartwheels at the chance to make "major" movies.

The filmmakers are incestuous; they star in each other's films and film each other's stars. There's a lot of simpatico between them—"You can bitch with each other about the struggles," says one of them—but there's a lot of sublimated antagonism, too, stemming from heavy-duty competition and the fact that certain of them reject association with any "underground" movement. Some feel they're better than the others. The rest know they're better than the others.

These are the Fassbinders, Schygullas and (God help us) Coppolas of tomorrow, but today they comprise a neglected, smoldering and complex downtown network. For many, they beg, borrow and work odd jobs. They build sets in their living rooms and glue cue cards onto the walls. For actors, they use the best that's available, meaning whoever works cheap and doesn't give attitude. "If you have a person living down the street from you who can play a part," said Israeli-born filmmaker Amos Poe a few years ago, "why go to the Actors Studio and find somebody there?"

Unlike the avant-garde films of such sixties' filmmakers as Stan Brackhage and Michael Snow—which were more about the medium of film itself than any particular subject—most underground films in the first half of the eighties are practically obsessed with narrative. Many are shameless melodramas that seem to have nothing at all to do with the blasé life south of St. Marks Place. Detective characters unravel life's sick, intriguing mysteries along with the filmmaker and the audience.

If Amos Poe's films are often about outsiders, maybe it's because he himself was one. He lived off Diesengorff Circle, which he calls the Times Square of Tel Aviv, until he was eight. Poe, who claims to have been sexually aroused for the first time when he saw Marilyn Monroe in *Niagara*, never intended to make films. After being expelled from college at eighteen, he found himself with a camera in Czechoslovakia in 1968, right before the Russian invasion, which he shot obsessively. He sold his photos to Time-Life, Inc., for a tidy sum, then realized he'd probably never find equally compelling photographic images. He turned to film.

The Blank Generation, which Poe made with kindred spirit Ivan Kral of Patti Smith's group, is a shabby concert film which has Talking Heads, Blondie, Smith and other CBGB regulars, singing and emoting while the soundtrack wails on totally out of sync. Made in 1975 with cassettes and a Super 8 camera, this "Puttin' on the Hits" gone haywire is a forerunner of the proud-to-be-shoddy wave. Eric Mitchell's Super 8's took the poverty aesthetic into even more dizzying heights. Said a peer, "You can barely see his films—they don't look like anything. He doesn't have the slightest idea of how the cameras work." Yet his films, like Poe's, are kind of mesmerizing, you'd have to say.

"We want to communicate to people," says Beth B. "I don't want to make something I can only show in my living room to people I know." "We're trying to make our work accessible to a large public," says Scott B., "and that's threatening to the idea of high art." "But we don't want to make high art," laughs Beth B.

The B's continue full force, and Nick Zodiac, who created the underground sci-fi classic *Geek Maggot Bingo* and *They Eat Scum*, which documented the takeover of New York by a band of cannibals, returned to take over the Limbo Lounge in 1985 with a Friday night film and performance series called "Theater of Shame." Mitchell came out with a full-fledged feature,

The Way It Is, shortly afterwards. A lot of these artists, though, haven't been heard of since the New Cinema closed. Some of them just changed directions midstream. From 1979 to 1981, Nares was the George Plimpton of everything he could get his hands on—he played guitar with the Contortions; collaborated on *X* magazine; did camerawork on John Lurie's Super 8, *Men in Orbit*; shot Johnston's *Sleepless Nights*, and played percussion with the Del Byzanteens. He's since, like seemingly everyone else, been mostly painting.

And what about the filmmaking survivors (organ music)? Will they ever cross over to mainstream Hollywood (drumroll, fadeout)? In 1979 actress Tina L'Hotsky ventured an opinion when she said, "These people are seedpods of potential growth, but they don't have money, so they'll never grow. They'll wither like weeds. There's no middle ground between the underground and Hollywood cinemas, so they'll always be 'attempt-istic.' "

But L'Hotsky's remark should be seen more as a perspective on that period than as a timeless damnation for anyone with a camera and little else. Since she said that, music video has opened up enormous possibilities, (Amos Poe, after co-writing and directing the $1.2 million film, *Alphabet City* has gone on to do videos for groups like Animotion and Van Zandt). And in film, a huge promising middle ground has been fertilized and grown.

Successful independents have not only come out of the scene but in many cases they've capitalized on some of its most appealing elements. Slava Tsuckerman's *Liquid Sky* (1983) cast some of New York's flashiest come-alive-at-night crowd in a sci-fi story that emphasized their ghoulishness. They were almost like George Romero zombies gone new wave, terrorizing clubs instead of shopping malls, and lending the film both fashion and fascination. The film featured striking model/actress Anne Carlisle, who in her dual male and female roles had the distinction of being the only actress in history to ever sleep with herself on screen.

Jarmusch's *Stranger Than Paradise* (1984) took the familiar outsider theme—"America as seen through the eyes of strangers," says the director—and gave it a downtown hipness and flipness. It cast three local darlings (John Lurie, Richard Edson and Eszter Balint) as a mismatched trio of outcast wanderers, always missing each other's connections in the drollest ways possible. Independent films don't have to pay attention to the usual ways of telling a story, and this one all but sent those usual ways flying into the cracked "Hollywood" sign. Scenes were presented as short blackouts, almost as in a vaudeville revue. Points of dramatic action were mostly not presented at all. The actors were encouraged to bring their own ideas to the characters yet never call attention to themselves as actors. The black-and-white cinematography, according to Jarmusch, was used to create the cumulative effect of a photo album. And the general intent was light years away from big, calculated dramas on the order of *Terms of Endearment*. "Films," says Jarmusch, "must find new ways of describing real emotions and real lives without manipulating the audience in the familiar, maudlin ways and without the recently fashionable elimination of all emotion." Though the characters talked in such schleppy tones you sometimes could barely hear them, when you did hear them, it usually had an impact—the ring of truth. Jarmusch is following *Paradise* up with a film about teenage love, which he says will be an answer to Hollywood's mindless teen-sex comedies. He's also working on a prison comedy called *Down By Law*, which is an answer to the inevitable question, "What's next for this indie boy wonder?"

We'll have to wait and see what an original talent like Jarmusch can do with more money: Will he make any sense in the land of dollars and cents? Seidelman's been snapped up by the moviedom mainstream, yet by holding out and not doing the *Porky's*-style locker-room farces that were offered to her, she made the move with integrity.

Charlie Ahearn, whose *Wild Style* made a minisplash in 1982, is one of the ascending indies and, as such, has experienced both the pros and cons of independence. On the one hand, he can avoid cinematic formulas and develop any idea he wants, but on the other, he has to be prepared to have a lot of doors slammed in his face. Doorknob wounds are part of being independent.

Indies are sometimes like those woefully amateur musicians standing on street corners with signs that say, "Starving Musician Needs Your Contribution to Get to Juilliard." You know very well that the only contribution that'll get them to Juilliard is a ninety-cent token, but that doesn't mean they'll be actually admitted into the school. Others of them genuinely do need just a little money and a lot of encouragement to get where they want to go. Ahearn falls into the latter category. With a million dollars and a pat on the back, he could probably outdo Steven Spielberg.

He lives where you'd expect him to, in the heart of Times Square's swirl of street life, exploitation flicks and nonstop, unrelenting real life. A mere block away from his apartment, you can revel in slices of life like *Splatter University* and *Zombie Island Massacre*, but at his place you're surrounded only by posters for *Wild Style*. He's proud of it. Crudely, almost rottenly done for a mere $300,000, the film's exploration of the graffiti and hip-hop culture caught on with a midnight audience before *Beat Street* was even a glimmer in Harry Belafonte's checkbook. The film starred Fun Gallery's Patti Astor as the scene outsider observing a graffitist like Zephyr, and features cameos by Grandmaster Flash, the Rock Steady Crew and others, with music by Chris Stein. Shoddy as it was, *Wild Style* was cool before hip-hop was cool.

Ahearn came to New York City from Binghamton, New York, in 1973, intending to be an artist, but found, "In the seventies, art was not what was happening." Instead, he got involved in making underground films—literally. "I went to the gold mines in Arizona with Scott and Beth B. in 1976 and filmed under the ground." Intercutting those scenes with closeups of a Catholic mass, which he got to shoot by telling the church he was part of a visiting brotherhood, Ahearn came up with a bizarre film that analogized the gold in the church with that in the mine. It was a bit pretentious, "Personal," he says, but it should be revived at Limelight or somewhere underground, maybe at Vito Bruno's next subway party.

Going from Catholic mass to mass appeal, Ahearn later did a full-length martial arts film, *The Deadly Art of Survival*, which enjoyed the best of both the under and above ground worlds. The film played the New Cinema and was also shown to a sold-out house at a more commercial space, the Orpheum on Second Avenue. "Martial arts is a real common denominator for the street," says Ahearn, who's not unlike a Keith Haring of film. He has just as much of a commercial egalitarian sense about him.

Influenced by everything from Buster Keaton to musical comedies, Ahearn's credits also include his movie *Twins*, about a guy who's trying to kill his policeman brother on their thirtieth birthday. That was a clever stroke of art imitating life; the idea was thought up by Ahearn's real-life twin brother, John.

It wasn't until *Wild Style*, though, that the quirkily intense filmaholic made the big push towards respectability. Amazingly, he came up with some TV presale money in Europe. "But even once I got the money together, it was incredibly hard to get a distributor. I didn't know what I was doing, whether the offers were good or bad. That's why it took me a year to get the film shown, and that's an absurdly long time when you consider that *Breakin'* was put together in a record four months or so."

Still, Ahearn can console himself with having his film, and his conscience intact. He's been established as someone with both street smarts and foresight. And the distributor says the film might even turn a profit soon.

● John Sex met "The Living Unicorn" at Area's Ringling Brothers' party that captivated downtown with its timeliness and absurdity. The two locked horns for the photographers, but came out friends.

Every time an underground filmmaker turns a profit, it's one more little victory for downtown, another chance to prove that creativity can mean solvency. It's cause for pom-pom girls, who should keep cheering whenever a starving painter sells a canvas or a band's demo tape finally leads to that dotted line.

Unfortunately, once the struggle that makes downtown so volatile dissolves into successful complacency, sometimes the creative spark dissolves, too, and the formerly underground segue a little too comfortably into the commercial world. That's the built-in catch 22 of downtown success. Once you're out of the scene, you no longer have the benefit of the trappings, freedom and drive that made you successful in the first place.

But no one's going to complain too loudly if it means recognition beyond the same old twelve-block radius. And the fact that outsiders have fixed on downtown for its commercial potential means it's easier for the scene's personalities to get their breaks and still keep their downtown ties if they want to.

The East Village life has become such an effective selling point way beyond 14th Street that one lime juice company used the image of an East Village artist—which, let's face it, has not much to do with lime juice—to sell its product. Tommy Gunn, a highly photogenic musician and club employee who looks like Prince gone haywire, was seen briefly on a Honda commercial as part of that company's constant striving for coolness. Dianne Brill and John Sex, naturals for the video medium if ever there were any, showed up in the Cars' "Hello Again" clip, directed by Andy Warhol, and ex-Palladium doorwoman Sally Randall, the bewigged hostess of many a not-so-humble chapeau, was sighted in a Run-D.M.C. video and called upon for frequent TV and print appearances.

Randall, who seems terribly blasé on the surface, masks an inner dynamism that extends to her gossip column writing, show producing and tireless self-promotion, all of which makes her the scene's most visible dilettante, choosing her next "star" move as carefully as her next outfits. If there was a time when it seemed like she was producing one or two fashion shows a week, it was because she was producing one or two fashion shows a week. Now every night is a fashion show for Sally; in a blinking belt, knee-length blond wig of the type Cyndi Lauper later adapted and skyscraper-sized leopard hat, she's one-of-a-kind. And it's the one-of-a-kinds that media tend to notice, because they're drawn to sheer visual power more readily than achievement. Sally, of course, strives for both. She's a role model for anyone who dreams of making nightlife into a career.

An unnoticed suburban girl, she transformed herself into "the demimonde's girl of the minute" using a mixture of accessories and smarts. Some worship her wackiness. Others say she has "all the depth and personality of a Lucite paperweight." Maybe they're just jealous of her seemingly effortless stride into notoriety. Don't they realize Sally has tremendous depth? (And height, too, thanks to her many wigs and hats.) She's also developed a devotion to music that has interested some backers, and just might have her laughing last. The Sally Randall legend is just beginning.

It's an eighties phenomenon that working a door didn't hurt her chances of getting noticed, or being liked ("Hi Sally. You look fabulous. I'm here with twelve guests"). The days when a doorperson was a powerful, but laughable object of contempt are now just faded memories from a nonexistent guest list. "Now, working the door is a valid career," says Stephen Saban, who remembers a time when that was not the case. (In fact, he remembers a lot; Fred Rothbell-Mista claims Saban's been around so long as he gave Cleopatra's sweet sixteen party). Not only is it a valid career, it's practically a steppingstone for stardom. Why are people wasting their time printing up resumes and head shots and singing "Feelings" at degrading off-Broadway auditions when they could just get a door job, stand on top of a box and bat their eyelashes until the big producers notice them?

While Randall was on her way to becoming a household hat, another Palladium worker was asked to be in a major director's next film, all based on the Oscar-caliber charisma she displayed in making a cocktail. Downtown is such a public spectacle that strokes of recognition like that are bound to happen. No less than two stars—movie actress Linda Fiorentino (*VisionQuest, After Hours*) and TV star Bruce Willis (*Moonlighting*)—were first noticed as starry-eyed club help at Kamikaze. And Saban went from checking the guest list there to heading it. Two parts personality, one part rum—and we're talking stardom, hold the parasol.

The downtown stars sometimes seem like the high school elite eight years later, still running the organizations, sneaking their arms around potential dates and hiding their report cards from their parents. Sally's the twirler captain, seemingly aloof, but full of vim and vigor on the field. Dianne Brill's the head cheerleader, personally cheering on each football player and designing costumes for the school show on the side. (She's also most likely to succeed, most popular girl, and the first one to show up at the senior prom). John Sex is the class clown, Stephen Saban the class scribe. Fred Rothbell-Mista is the morale booster who could even outboost Brill. Keith Haring's the one who, instead of dissecting the frog on bio lab, turns it into a diorama. Alan Rish wants to throw a party for the diorama.

Teri Toye and Jean Michel Basquiat won't sign anyone's yearbook and Oliver Rish, Alan's ultranice socialite cousin, is the one who writes, "You're 2 Good 2 Be 4-Gotten." John Lurie plays sax in the bathroom during the three minutes between classes and Andy Anderson's the one who comes in and puts invitations in the mouth of the sax. Peter Gatien's the assistant principal you hardy ever see. Steve Rubell's the head principal you always see.

This isn't like high school in that no one's grading you, except your peers. There are no academic obligations. No one's keeping you there for four years or forcing you to leave after four years. No, it isn't high school. But just like in high school, there are certain most-likelies who dominate everything. Just like in high school, these same people assume they've reached the pinnacle of success just because they've made a few friends and influenced people and been involved in a few minor events. The social survival principle stayed pretty much the same. Back then, the trick was to put on enough attitude to impress your classmates all the way through to the very boring graduation ceremony, at which point you were horrifyingly on your own.

Similarly, the trick now is to achieve the kind of stardom that won't have you showing up in those "Whatever happened to . . . ?" books in the amount of time it would take to erase your name from one of those computerized mailing lists. It's been said that a journalist can create an art star, but the same journalist can undo all his star making merely by never mentioning that artist again. The stars, unfortunately, never realize that they should minimize their stellar attitude until after their downfall. As one club manager said about a former protégé who went on to media saturation and all its concomitant snobbery, "If she says goodbye to me on the way up, I'm not saying hello to her on the way down." Good riddance to bad rubbish and all that, and don't let the doorknob hit you on the way out.

Better to be a bona fide star for the duration than ride the crest of a particular wave only to crash with it when it's pressed into history books. Most of the Studio 54 luminaries probably wouldn't even get into the hot clubs right now without a bit of a battle; like butterflies under a sun-drenched magnifying glass, they're singed for life.

The real downtown stars don't walk around saying, "Hi. I'm a downtown star." They don't run up to photographers, spin on their heads and whistle "Dixie." They don't say they're the heirs to the Woolworth fortune, but could they please borrow $20 while they're waiting for the inheritance to clear. Those are the fake downtown stars, and there are a lot of them. The real ones cut through the flash and spectacle with startling substance. Everything they do—from social gestures to arm gestures—is a potential fashion statement or work of art. The self-made oddities make downtown a fun place to visit, but these true stars make it a great place to live.

10

And the Beat Goes On »

Not only has the St. Marks Cinema caved in to gentrification, but for a while even its "Closed For Renovation" announcement seemed to be crumbling. The Cinema is being converted into stores, a living testament to the reigning dichotomy of downtown—commercialization attempting to take over as East Village life continues to defiantly parade through. If real estate agents force these defiant ones out of their neighborhood, they'll just change their addresses, but not their style.

Unlike some of the past underground stars and movements that ended up assuming unpleasant positions in gutters and are now remembered only by morbid historians, the current crop will only assume positions of power no one will forget. The creative energy of downtown and its people (and new recruits) will keep the scene going even when the media decide it's no longer worth their rapt attention. The difference is that downtown luminaries *want* to "crossover." They *want* to live in the "real" world. Ann Magnuson, for all her artiness, aspires above all else to be the star of a TV sitcom. Dianne Brill would like nothing better than to be recognized as a peer on Seventh Avenue. John Sex's fondest wish is to play Carnegie Hall—though probably not in a traditional tux. These people can laugh at Yuppies all they want—it's healthy to laugh at yourself. But why shouldn't the creative fringes have career ambitions too? The real heros of downtown are the artists who manage to keep one foot firmly planted in their roots and the other foot moving towards upward mobility. Laurie Anderson, Keith Haring and Jim Jarmusch come to mind.

The scene will probably become more genuine when it's not being paraded around for the *Entertainment Tonight* audience to get a rise. Once the thrill of discovery wears off, so will the pressures of trendiness and the clamoring of the phonies desperate to be a part of it. The true-blue downtowners who find the swirl of fun and fashion addicting will keep it alive with their constant input of irreverent, yet highly pragmatic self-reinvention. They'll create for the sake of it, not for the notoriety it now inevitably attracts. People like Rudolf, who says every club will be his last, will continue opening clubs. Stephen Sprouse will continue designing, Robert Molnar will always keep his hand in fashion—even though he recently closed his showroom—and Tish and Snooky Bellomo will always be involved in some creative entreprenurial endeavor or other. The Whiners will keep on whining, too.

If downtown can survive the trendiness ascribed to it in a potentially deadly way, it will emerge even more glisteningly alive than it is now. Unfortunately, that trendiness seems to be seeping into every crevice of the downtown environs, threatening the self-contained quality that originally gave the scene its dynamism and originality. In October 1985, *The East Village Eye* declared that neighborhood's art scene officially dead, a casualty of the media overkill surrounding it. It's hard for artists to take their neighborhood seriously when there are street photographers posing tourists against East Village backdrops so they can impress the folks back home with snapshots of their wild New York experience. The writing on the wall will be even more legible if concession stands start selling East Village keychains and snowdomes.

But those things will only spell the end of downtown's unofficial headquarters, not downtown itself. If St. Marks Place turns into a shiny, high tech equivalent of a suburban mall, the scene will hardly be reduced to a series of glossy sushi restaurants. It's too resilient and big to be bound by geographical parameters and besides, the gentrification battle will probably make all the creative artists even more fiercely determined to survive. If they can fight for free drinks, they can certainly fight for their neighborhood.

Meanwhile, the trendiness will not only encourage a proliferation of unsightly tourists, it'll contribute to the flash-in-the-pan nature of some of the downtown talent. The Fun Gallery and Stephen Sprouse, for example, probably could have both prolonged their success if they hadn't been swept into it so quickly and unexpectedly and leaped upon by trendies who forced them into situations requiring business smarts they just didn't have. Future downtowners will be forearmed with the wisdom those people earned the hard way.

They'll be shrewder than ever, knowing that they can be as wild as they want, as long as they're as wild as the mass market wants. While past ground-breakers practically stared self-destruction in the face with every creative leap, these kids are more careful, with less to be mad about and more to get ahead for—like the spiralling cost of living.

It's doubtful that designers will create extreme statements on a par with the punk movement, mainly because they have less opposition to create a statement against. So, fashions will continue to be colorful, sassy and fun—personal more than social statements—with an eye towards wearability and versatility so the clothes will be worn by more than just zanies-on-a-spree.

Most of the businesspeople who opened a gallery or boutique in hopes of jumping on a trend will fail because the East Village knows when it's being exploited. Even some of the sincere ones will fail, but their creative drive will find them a place somewhere in this receptive anti-culture. Bandwagon-hopping can only last so long before business reality sets in. When entrepreneurs realize they need some substance behind their crumbling facades to make it for more than a month, galleries will stop turning up every time a shoe store closes. East Villagers will once again have places to fix their shoes.

Once the unworthy galleries are weeded out, the East Village art world will be relieved of some of its dilettantish stigma, though one hopes that the edge that gives it its raison d'etre will never dissolve into the edge of night. Art dealers will continue to search for the "overnights" to make up for the ones that took even less time to move on, but they'll have to look even harder for lasting talents because the flashes only satisfy the pool of buyers until the paint is dry. That pool will continue to expand and increase in sophistication and their cravings will become gargantuan. And though the East Village artists will still veer wildly from brightly kitschy to darkly disturbing ("Tortured Lost Souls Burning Forever!" was the ad line for a recent exhibit), the angsty contingent will probably shrink as the scene grows more comfortable. Once they start selling their paintings, there'll be a lot less to complain about.

Downtown musicians and performance artists will take even greater advantage of the video medium (and vice versa), where all their visual lunacy can be copiously mined. They'll also find that their reliance on familiar pop genres will count as a plus as long as they can rework those genres into fresh-sounding material that's not too intimidating. Though the Lounge Lizards will probably never have a Top 10 hit, it's not hard to imagine the Fabulous Pop Tarts permeating the airwaves, Zette becoming a MTV star or *Mermaids on Heroin* making it as a staple on the midnight movie circuit, if not earlier.

Independent filmmakers will continue to wake Hollywood up to the fact that you don't need forty million dollars to produce a decent film or twenty million to make a bomb. They'll bring more and more downtown actors and personalities to the attention of an increasingly large and willing audience who'll want to know more about the scenes they've already had a look at in *Desperately Seeking Susan* and Martin Scorsese's *After Hours*.

Clubs will continue to open and close in don't-blink-or-you'll-miss-'em succession, and while none will top Palladium for sheer spectacle, some will inevitably cater more exclusively to downtown, giving the Fabulous 500 homier places to hang their fabulous hats, like that dairy-colored palace of informality, the MilkBar. Some clubs might even respond to Palladium's grandeur by going to the opposite extreme and creating themselves more in the image of starker, intimate hangouts *a la* Mudd. But the growing legion of scenemakers—Steve Rubell estimates that there are now 45,000 New Yorkers going to clubs as opposed to 5,500 when Studio 54 opened—will demand a large variety of nightlife possibilities at least as vast as the current array. And they'll want the grandiose places to be among their choices, because they've been spoiled by the splendor of it all.

Palladium was supposed to shorten the distance from which downtown and uptown ogle each other. That club was originally billed as a revolutionary advance in crowd selection, an unprecedented mix of up and down. Except that though there *are* uptowners and downtowners there, it seems as if all the uptowners stay downstairs to dance while the downtowners migrate to mix and mingle in the Mike Todd Room ("Cream always rises . . ."), with few brazen adventurers from each camp crossing over to the other territory without the ammunition of courage and un-self-consciousness. As clubs get bigger, there'll be even more room for uptown and downtown people to polarize in. It's up to their own initiative to break the magnetic field.

The clubs that offer unpretentious good times—Danceteria, Limelight, Pyramid—could conceivably go on forever with their unlikely mixes of people. They're not part of any trend other than the fun-in-nightlife trend, which will never die.

And no matter where downtowners hang out, there will always be a downtown, a place where you can be accepted for daring to be different. New scenemakers will come in and change the hierarchy, but there'll always be room for anyone with a dream and an outfit, a party drive and a talent—or three or four—worth partying and daring to be different about.

About the Author »

Michael Musto writes the weekly nightlife and entertainment column "La Dolce Musto" in *The Village Voice*. He is the film critic for *Saturday Review* and writes about the arts for *Details*, *Us* and *Interview* magazines. Mr. Musto's play, *Hollywood Hell (or Cute Doesn't Age Well)* was performed at New York's Theater for the New City. His neo-Motown group, Michael Musto and the Must, is represented on SONY's video E.P. *Danspak II*.

Photo Credits

Page

1.	PATRICK MCMULLAN	74.	WOLFGANG WESENER
3.	BEN BUCHANAN	79.	PATRICK MCMULLAN
6.	KATE SIMON	80.	WOLFGANG WESENER
8.	PATRICK MCMULLAN	83.	PATRICK MCMULLAN
11.	MARCIA RESNICK	90.	PATRICK MCMULLAN
14.	BOB GRUEN	92.	RICHARD BOWDITCH
23.	PATRICK MCMULLAN	96.	LISA STEIN
27.	BEN BUCHANAN	101.	ROBIN PLATZER
31.	PATRICK MCMULLAN	104.	BEN BUCHANAN
35.	BEN BUCHANAN	106–107.	WOLFGANG WESENER
39.	BEN BUCHANAN	110.	WOLFGANG WESENER
43.	BEN BUCHANAN	115.	ROBIN PLATZER
47.	WOLFGANG WESENER	120.	PATRICK MCMULLAN
50.	WOLFGANG WESENER	123.	BEN BUCHANAN
53.	WOLFGANG WESENER	129.	ROBIN PLATZER
59.	PATRICK MCMULLAN	131.	ROBIN PLATZER
62.	ROBIN PLATZER	139.	ROBIN PLATZER
64.	BEN BUCHANAN	141.	ROBIN PLATZER
66.	WOLFGANG WESENER	155.	BEN BUCHANAN
68.	PATRICK MCMULLAN	159.	BEN BUCHANAN